"*The Coach's Way* is possibly the finest resource available for anyone who wants to develop or enrich their coaching abilities. This new book is designed to give coaches the confidence and structure in their practice that will generate real results for their clients. Anyone who makes a living in the coaching arena will benefit from Dr. Maisel's tremendous experience and training as a therapist, coach, and human. I'm so glad to have this book as a guide for my own coaching work and will recommend it to many others in the helping professions."

— **Jacob Nordby**, author of *The Creative Cure: How Finding and Freeing Your Inner Artist Can Heal Your Life*

"Sharing decades of experience as a coach, Eric has succinctly captured the very essence of *what* it means to coach someone as a professional coach, and more importantly, *how* to hold space for a coachee. Because of that, this book will no doubt join the archives of classic books that new coaches will rely on when it comes to understanding how a coaching session can be a beautiful, easy, intimate, cooperative, and highly useful conversation — even a magical one."

— from the foreword by **Dawn Campbell**, business director, International Authority for Professional Coaching and Mentoring (IAPC&M)

"*The Coach's Way* invites us to make an agreement to bring our true self as a human being into coaching and to wholeheartedly hold the intention to help another person. Eric Maisel unpacks the nuances, mystery, and practical skills of the coaching session itself, offering tips for success and a strong helping process. As coaches, we are called upon in this book to live a life of meaning and purpose and to help our clients do the same. I have practiced as a coach for over two decades now and trained in many different coaching modalities. I highly recommend this book to coaches at any stage of their lives and work!"

— **Lynda Monk**, MSW, RSW, CPCC,
life, wellness, and creativity coach and director of
International Association for Journal Writing

"Eric Maisel has coached me for over ten years, playing a huge role in guiding me to success as a novelist and a creativity coach. Maisel has an extremely wide knowledge base and brings his potent coaching style of deep listening and inquiry, encouragement, and wisdom to each coaching session. *The Coach's Way* promises a broad and deep exploration of the subject of coaching, with Maisel's unique approach shining through. This is a must-read for anyone interested in the wonderful process of coaching!"

— **Eva Weaver**, coach and author of
The Puppet Boy of Warsaw and *The Eye of the Reindeer*

THE
COACH'S
WAY

Also by Eric Maisel

Redesign Your Mind

Rethinking Depression

Secrets of a Creativity Coach

*60 Innovative Cognitive
Strategies for the Bright,
the Sensitive, and the Creative*

Sleep Thinking

Ten Zen Seconds

Toxic Criticism

*Transformational Journaling for
Coaches, Therapists, and Clients*
(editor, with Lynda Monk)

20 Communication Tips at Work

*20 Communication Tips for
Families*

Unleashing the Artist Within

The Van Gogh Blues

What Would Your Character Do?

Why Smart People Hurt

Why Smart Teens Hurt

Write Mind

A Writer's Paris

A Writer's San Francisco

A Writer's Space

FICTION

Aster Lynn

The Black Narc

The Blackbirds of Mulhouse

Dismay

The Fretful Dancer

*The Girl with the Collaborator
Sister*

The Kingston Papers

Murder in Berlin

Settled

JOURNALS

Artists Speak

Writers and Artists on Devotion

Writers and Artists on Love

MEDITATION DECKS

Everyday Calm

Everyday Creative

Everyday Smart

THE COACH'S WAY

The Art and Practice of Powerful Coaching in Any Field

ERIC MAISEL

Foreword by Dawn Campbell

New World Library
Novato, California

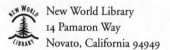

New World Library
14 Pamaron Way
Novato, California 94949

Text design by Tona Pearce Myers

Library of Congress Cataloging-in-Publication Data

Names: Maisel, Eric, date, author.
Title: The coach's way : the art and practice of powerful coaching in any field / Eric Maisel ; foreword by Dawn Campbell.
Description: Novato, California : New World Library, [2023] | Summary: "Reveals how an experienced creativity coach and former psychotherapist conducts coaching sessions that make a difference in the lives of his clients. This workshop-in-a-book will benefit professional coaches of all kinds, as well as managers, team leaders, teachers, or anyone who informally mentors others"-- Provided by publisher.
Identifiers: LCCN 2023000784 (print) | LCCN 2023000785 (ebook) | ISBN 9781608688647 (paperback) | ISBN 9781608688654 (epub)
Subjects: LCSH: Personal coaching. | Psychology, Applied. | Creative ability.
Classification: LCC BF637.P36 M34 2023 (print) | LCC BF637.P36 (ebook) | DDC 158.3--dc23/eng/20230209
LC record available at https://lccn.loc.gov/2023000784
LC ebook record available at https://lccn.loc.gov/2023000785

First printing, April 2023
ISBN 978-1-60868-864-7
Ebook ISBN 978-1-60868-865-4
Printed in Canada on 100% postconsumer-waste recycled paper

New World Library is proud to be a Gold Certified Environmentally Responsible Publisher. Publisher certification awarded by Green Press Initiative.

10   9   8   7   6   5   4   3   2   1

For Ann, forty-five years into this adventure

Contents

WEEK 12. ON PROGRESS ◆ 169

WEEK 13. THE WORK OVER TIME ◆ 184

Foreword

A central tenet of Taoism is naturalness. The "way" in Taoism has to do with ease, spontaneity, and connection, that there is an eternal, nameless, indescribable, but nevertheless authentic path that each of us can walk. It is a path that coachees choose to walk together with their coaches, which is an honor and responsibility that coaches do not take lightly.

Confucius added a humanistic overlay to the Tao by marrying the ideas of virtue and humanity and conceiving of the Tao as a humanistic path. When a writer uses the phrase "the way" to name what he or she is describing, there is an implied connection to these ancient ideas of ease, naturalness, connection, virtue, and what it means to be human.

This is what Eric Maisel, a master coach and popular masterclass speaker at the International Authority for Professional Coaching & Mentoring (IAPC&M), has achieved with *The Coach's Way*, his latest in a long line of well-thought-out, user-friendly, practical books.

Sharing decades of experience as a coach, Eric has succinctly captured the very essence of *what* it means to coach someone as a professional coach, and more importantly, *how* to hold space for a coachee. Because of that, this book will no doubt join the archives of classic books that new coaches will rely on when it comes to understanding how a coaching session can be a beautiful, easy, intimate, cooperative, and highly useful conversation — even a magical one.

Coaching, when conducted well, touches the soul of a coachee and uncovers what they want to be, do, and have in their personal and professional lives. As a director at the IAPC&M, I hear all too often from recently certified coaches, proudly clutching their certificates, the question of "What now? How do I turn my training investment into a heartfelt coaching practice?" Eric's book answers that question, lesson by lesson, as he effortlessly takes coaches working in the humanist tradition through the process of managing a successful coaching session.

IAPC&M coaches sign our Professional Code of Conduct, making it clear that, because they are working with a coachee's mind, they must commit to ensuring that their coachees' mental health and well-being are protected. The coach sits with another human being, maybe in the same room or maybe remotely, with the aim to be there in that moment, fully awake, alive, and present to what the coachee is saying, honoring the humanist ideals of truth, beauty, and goodness. This is not science but basic humanity.

A coach is a human experience specialist, someone who knows what human beings feel, think, encounter, and experience as they navigate personal life and professional goals. A coach knows that human beings sometimes despair; that they sometimes rise to the occasion; that they sometimes don't; that they sometimes make themselves proud by their efforts; that they sometimes disappoint themselves. This is a coach's area of expertise, along with whatever other specialized knowledge they bring to a coaching session. It is a special way of two people being deeply and poignantly together; and, for the coachee, it is often a first-time experience of being so deeply seen and heard.

What happens on this "way"? Open, powerfully thought-provoking, and results-oriented questions are asked. Investigations commence. Feelings are aired honestly. Silence falls. Challenges, obstacles, and excuses are explored. Limiting beliefs are reframed. Silence falls again. Plans get hatched. Cheerleading occurs. There is a naturalness and spontaneity to what goes on in this unique relationship of exploration, silence, reflection, accountability, and empowerment.

With an experienced coach, it occurs without a whiff of script or theory and has more to do with intuition backed up by experience and deep listening. Sessions are very much a shared effort and a shared experience between two equals who are committed to making a positive difference.

This book focuses on *professional coaches*: coaches who are properly trained, coaches who are insured (*if* their country offers insurance), coaches who are logging their coaching hours and are committed to continuing professional development, and increasingly, coaches who are independently accredited and are supported through supervision. That said, coaching is by any other name just a great conversation, so *The Coach's Way* will no doubt speak to everyone in a helping relationship: parents, mental health counselors, human resources specialists, teachers, tutors, mentors, spouses. Who doesn't need to help someone sometimes?

So, you could say that this book is for everyone committed to improving their lives through improved communication skills. In a sense that is what I hope you will come to appreciate and understand: that "the coach's way" is really everyone's way. I hope you will enjoy this book as much as I have and that its magic rubs off on your coaching practice as you go about helping your coachees. And if you're not a coach, you and those around you will still benefit!

Dawn Campbell
Business Director, International Authority for
Professional Coaching & Mentoring
(https://coach-accreditation.services)

Introduction

I've been sitting across from folks and trying to help them for a very long time now, going on forty years. All we do is talk, and you might not think that talk could amount to very much by way of help. But it can. Dr. Martin Luther King Jr.'s "I Have a Dream" speech was just talk, after all. It didn't have the power of law; it wasn't a medical intervention; it couldn't make friends out of enemies. It was just some words, right? Not hardly.

When you're sitting across from another person as a helper, your only apparent tool is words. But you can nevertheless function as a genuine change agent. By virtue of your presence, your thoughtfulness, your suggestions, your very way of being and engaging, you can help a person live the life she wants to live, the life she hasn't been able to manifest or achieve on her own. All you have at your disposal are your attitude, your wisdom, and some words — but put those all together, and you can be of powerful help.

In this book, I'll explain how that remarkable thing, a coaching session, can function at its best — and how it can do so while also being easy on the coach. It is important that a coach find the work she does more effortless than exhausting, or else she will quickly burn out. Coaching really can be easy and effortless, if you follow the field-tested practices I'll be presenting. If you give my ideas a try, I think you'll discover that coaching may be exactly the right profession for you.

People are challenged in all sorts of ways — by poor health, by economic realities, by political events, by existential and spiritual crises, by career shortfalls, by creative blockages, by relationship difficulties. Coaching can help with each of these problems. Of course, a coach can't snap her fingers and wave difficulties away. But she can support the person across from her as, together, they unravel those knotty difficulties and cocreate the best solutions possible. Coaching isn't a magic bullet, but it can be rather magically useful.

The goals of this book are to provide you with a good sense of what coaching is all about, to help you design and launch your own coaching practice, and to paint a picture of how coaching can be easy rather than arduous. I've called this book *The Coach's Way* because I wanted to suggest how coaching can be a natural and effortless sort of thing. I also wanted the lessons to match that vision of ease, so each lesson is short and comes with exercises that begin with the supereasy.

My hope is that you will engage with the exercises at the end of each lesson. This book is made up of lessons that take hardly twenty minutes to absorb and are meant to fit into your real day and your real life. The idea is to tackle one lesson a day over the course of thirteen weeks, taking the time to do one or more of the exercises provided. Please try at least one of those exercises for each lesson — the easy ones also count!

If you're a professional coach or thinking of becoming one, this book will speak to you directly. Even if you're someone who doesn't coach for a living — if you're a psychotherapist, a mental health counselor, a teacher, a workshop leader, a manager — you, too, will benefit from these lessons. Knowing how to sit across from a person, whether that person is a high school student, a therapy client, or an employee, and apply the principles of coaching that I describe in this book will help you do your job both more easily and more effectively. No matter what your field, these lessons will serve you.

Many people who would enjoy coaching and who would make an effective coach never do it, even if they train as one. There are reasons for this avoidance, and I hope that this book helps you override any reluctance you may have. I would love it if it provided you with the impetus to launch, resume, or deepen your coaching practice. People in need of help are waiting, and you could be of real support to them. I hope that you'll invite them into your world!

1

You Are You

You are somebody, not everybody and not nobody.

The way this is customarily said is that you have a "personality." Maybe you are more introverted or more extroverted, more confident or less confident, more wounded by past experiences or less wounded, more of a worrier or more of a doer. Whatever the exact details, you are you, a particular member of a certain species with a certain genetic history, certain experiences, certain attitudes, certain proclivities, all coming together as the thing we call "personality."

You and I haven't traveled the same path. I am a retired family therapist and active coach; you may have a teaching credential, a certificate as a yoga trainer, or experiences as a shaman. You and I do not have the same genetic code, the same wiring, the same cellular memories, the same style of indwelling. You may love something I hate, and I may love something you hate. Isn't that obviously true? But as obvious as that is, we need to say it out loud, remember it, and honor it.

You are not me. You are you. It's been said (I think I remember it from the cop show *Blue Bloods*) that each of us has three lives: a public life, a private life, and a secret life. I've written about personality as being comprised of three parts: original personality, formed personality, and available personality. There are more ways than you can shake a stick at to conceptualize and describe "personality." The simple headline? When you sit across from a client in a coaching session, *you* will be there, in all your richness, strangeness, brightness, and shadowiness. You will have brought your personality with you.

Coaching begins with *you*. That is unavoidable.

What does this mean? Why am I bringing this up first? Because it is too easy to start talking about techniques, tactics, principles, and philosophies and to forget that coaching is a *human enterprise* and not a *technical enterprise*. When your child scrapes her knee, you approach the moment first of all as a parent, not as a first aid worker, though you may be that also. First you kneel and commiserate and care. Then you pull out the ointment and the Band-Aid.

"Mastering the coaching session" has a technical ring to it, as in, "First you do this, and then you do that." And there are certainly tactics and techniques to consider. But the picture you want to have in mind is of two people sitting across from each other, in person or remotely, both very human, both very complicated, both with needs, both ready to dive in, and both ready to bolt. This is not a person, the client, sitting across from a robot, the coach. Maybe that is coming…but right now coaching is still an encounter between two people, each with a history and a personality.

Accept that *you* will be there. Not some expert version of you, though you will gain expertise over time, but the current you, the constant you, the you that your Aunt Maisie would recognize as you, the you who prefers peach pie to apple pie and has trouble sleeping. Accept this reality, because there is no other. Yes, over time you may discern how to adopt a useful persona, a coaching persona. But who will have discerned that and adapted that to his or her needs and specifications? *You.*

EXERCISES

Easy. Visualize yourself sitting across from another person, preparing to be of help. See *you*, not some facsimile of you. What are you wearing? How does your hair look? There you are!

Easy. Say, "I can't avoid bringing me to the coaching session. Given that I can't avoid it, I accept — and embrace — that reality."

Medium. Accept that you, warts and all, opinions and all, prejudices and all, doubts and all, will be coming to the coaching session. Is there some ceremony to enact or some visualization to create that will help you accept that reality?

High bar. How can you bring the best of you to each session and avoid bringing the worst of you to each session? Give this question some thought.

Food for Thought for Informal Coaches

Do you do much informal coaching? Maybe you do, but hadn't really thought of it as coaching. Think of those times when you patiently tried to be of a little help to another person, maybe just by listening or maybe by offering suggestions. Do some such situations come to mind?

Writing Prompt for Self-Coaches

It is often easier to coach others than to coach ourselves, because when it comes to coaching ourselves, our own personality can get in the way. Write to the prompt "In order to coach myself, I am going to have to look out for…"

2

Decide for Yourself

Throughout this book, you'll hear me say, "You might try this" or even "Do this." All these pronouncements mean is that such-and-such has worked for me and suits my temperament and my outlook. But you must decide if it's suitable for *you*. Try not to suppose that there is a system or a method out there that will relieve you of the burden of figuring out for yourself how you want to be in session and what actually helps another person. No — that is every coach's burden.

If you are looking for a system or a method, you may take my pronouncements too seriously. Many coaches are uncomfortable as coaches, or even avoid coaching, because they get caught somewhere between wanting a method that works and wanting to trust themselves. Try not to get caught on that particular fence. Take in what I have to say, but opt to go your own way.

If you're a doctor, following a method that works is a really good idea. If you're a coach, however, the matter comes down to two principles: the principle of genuinely trying to be of help and the principle of being yourself. Try to move from "I'm not enough" or "I don't know enough" or "I don't have enough tools" or "I have no idea what to do" to the supersimple, friction-free, and ultimately effortless place of "I can just be me, and I can be of some help."

Take my pronouncements with a grain of salt. If you find that you are taking them too seriously, "kill the Buddha" by putting this book aside, finding a mirror, looking in that mirror, and saying, "I can just be me, and I can be of some help." Mean it when you say it. If you don't quite mean it — if you have your doubts — try some alternate phrase, like "I can find the way to be of help" or "I will grow into a great coaching persona." Look in the mirror and find the way to affirm yourself and to affirm your future.

Consider the great heavyweight champion Rocky Marciano, who fought some fearsome heavyweights (like Joe Louis) and retired undefeated. Marciano stood five foot ten inches tall, weighed 185 pounds, and had the shortest reach of any heavyweight in boxing history. Would it have made any sense for him to adopt a method or style that didn't suit his exact size, shape, and circumstances? No. To succeed, Marciano needed to crouch, fight inside, and keep himself in better shape than all of his competitors, so that he could still come out punching in the fifteenth round.

Likewise, you must create your way. Let's divide your coaching life into two parts: the beginning and all the rest. In the beginning, you may well want to try out suggestions of the sort that I make in this book, because, well, they have worked for me and for other coaches. In the beginning, it makes sense to allow yourself to be more the student than the master. But even in those early days and those first sessions, keep track of what works for you and how you might want to modify your tactics according to what you see happening. Then, make those changes.

You have not been handed your coaching self — you will need to create it. And you will, if you can find the courage to sit across from clients and learn from those real-life encounters.

EXERCISES

Easy. Say, "I will decide what sort of coach I want to be."

Easy. Say, "I get to create my own brilliant coaching persona."

Medium. Think about those times when you effectively and appropriately went your own way. What are your takeaways from those experiences?

High bar. Consider your personality. What parts of your personality are likely to serve you in session, and what parts aren't? For each of those parts that you suspect might not serve you very well, try to think through what you might do to lessen their impact.

Food for Thought for Informal Coaches

Picture an informal coaching situation — say, when you are coaching a team member at work and helping him deal with a work problem or a life problem. What sort of coach would you like to be? In your mind's eye, try out different coaching styles and see which one feels and fits best.

Writing Prompt for Self-Coaches

Write to the prompt "I can bring the following strengths to self-coaching..."

3

The First Agreement

A coaching session is first of all an agreement you make with yourself that you are willing to coach another human being. You are agreeing to risk-taking, vulnerability, effort, pushback, small panics, resistance, and all those other goblins that make you not really want to interact professionally with clients. When you make this agreement, you are agreeing to sweats, difficult silences … it is a long list of challenges that you are agreeing to. Have you made that agreement with yourself?

You may find this an easy agreement to make or even an agreement that you have already automatically made outside of conscious awareness. But many coaches *never seek out clients* because they haven't made this fundamental agreement with themselves: that they are willing to sit across from someone and coach him or her. They haven't made this fundamental agreement *to put themselves on the line*. Have you?

Your coaching sessions will reflect this lack of agreement in all sorts of negative ways, from the sessions exhausting you to your secret hope that clients will cancel. Your work for today is to reach this agreement with yourself.

This agreement might sound like: "I agree to coach actual human beings."

Or: "I can't wait to be of help!"

Or: "I am fully committed to being there for other people."

How might you say it?

I'm very aware of the statistics showing how difficult it is for human beings to follow through on their intentions. For instance, it's reported that 97 percent of folks who begin writing a book never finish it. That's quite a number. Maybe you thought that following through was much easier than that — that most other people were following through on their goals, dreams, and intentions. Well, that doesn't look to be the case.

So let us grab that bull by the horns and really agree that you are willing to sit across from another human being and coach him or her. You're going to lead, follow, make suggestions, weather push-back, and all the rest. Are we agreed?

Maybe a ceremony will help cement this agreement. Place two chairs facing each other. Sit on one. Imagine someone sitting on the other. Smile. Say hello. Ask some opening question, like "What's on your mind?" or, if you've been working together for a while, "Catch me up a little." Sit there comfortably. Lean a little forward, listen, be curious, feel energetic. As you do this, percolate the thought "Okay, I can do this. This is just fine. I can commit to this!"

You will actually seek out clients and your sessions will improve dramatically if you, maybe for the first time, agree that you are okay entering the life of another person, including folks who may prove difficult, and being with that person through his or her ups and downs. This is the first agreement, the fundamental agreement, and the one I hope that you can make right now.

Do you agree? See if you can find the courage, confidence, and wherewithal to agree. If you can, exclaim, "I agree!" What a wonderful ring that has to it!

EXERCISES

Easy. Whether or not you quite mean it or quite believe it, say, "I agree to coach!"

Medium. Journal to the prompt "I am reluctant to coach because…"

Medium. Journal to the prompt "Even though I am a little scared to coach, I will…"

High bar. Turn this agreement into the action step of recruiting clients to coach.

Food for Thought for Informal Coaches

Do you tend to avoid informal coaching situations because they feel risky or because you don't know what to do? For the sake of helping others, and maybe so as to help yourself in the process, do you want to internally agree to coach, even if that feels risky?

Writing Prompt for Self-Coaches

Write to the prompt "I know that self-coaching feels risky, because I risk disappointing myself by setting goals and not achieving them and for other reasons as well. But self-coaching is still worth pursuing, because…"

4

The Second Agreement

The second agreement is the pact you make with yourself that you intend to be of help. That you intend to be of help sounds obvious enough, but it's all too easy to come to a coaching session with a different agenda in mind — or in your heart.

Maybe you are smart and like to demonstrate that you are smart. That is a different agenda. Maybe you are needy and need something from your client, like approval. That is a different agenda. Maybe you are bossy and opinionated and want to make sure that your client gets an earful. That is a different agenda.

Do you agree that your central agenda is to be of some help?

There is a certain kind of offer of help that is polite, guarded, and not really an offer of help at all. Say that you enter a bank for a loan. The loan officer says, "How can I be of help?" But in actuality she has no intention of being of help if, for instance, you don't have the right collateral for a loan or otherwise don't meet her criteria for borrowing. She has said the right thing, but both of you know the rules of this game. She will be of help only if it suits her agenda.

Then there is a very different offer of help, say, when you see someone struggling to carry too many grocery bags. There, you really do mean, "Can I be of help?" when and if you say that. You are fully expecting to be of some carrying help. You are also clear that if this struggling person refuses your help, that is up to him. You are not presuming that your offer will be accepted, and you will not feel insulted or unappreciated if it isn't. You are making your kind offer without attachments and without expectations. You will be of some real help if your offer is accepted, and you will smile and walk away if it is refused.

Feel the difference between these two scenarios. It may seem a little odd to think of your client as coming to a coaching session as if carrying too many groceries, but it's an interesting image to conjure. First, you agreed to be there. There you are. That was your first agreement with yourself. Second, you are agreeing to be of help, as, say, a good Samaritan might be of help. You steady yourself in place and ready yourself to help.

Just as a parent possesses a wide range of helping behaviors — among them listening, teaching, reminding, inquiring, suggesting, and nodding — so a coach will develop a wide range of helping tactics in order to actually be of some help. Your toolbox will fill nicely, even beautifully, once you're committed to helping.

EXERCISES

Easy. Say, "I intend to be of help." Say it until it deeply registers.

Easy. Picture being with a friend and being of some help. Picture what that looks like and how that feels.

Medium. Why might you not want to be of help? What might get in the way?

High bar. Call to mind some times in your life when you were helped by someone. What sort of help was offered? Why did that help work?

Food for Thought for Informal Coaches

Picture approaching informal coaching situations, not as someone who knows things, but as someone who intends to be of help. Can you feel that difference?

Writing Prompt for Self-Coaches

Write to the prompt "I think I have these unconscious reasons for not wanting to be of help to myself…"

5

Relaxation

When you coach, you and your client occupy a certain space and spend a certain amount of time together. You want to relax into that space and relax into that time.

If you find it hard to relax around another person — whether it's at a cocktail party, with your parents, at work with coworkers, with your active child (the one always doing something dangerous), or even with a friend — then this becomes a first-order priority: a new, more relaxed way of being.

Can you become a more relaxed you? There are other ways of saying this: Can you become a less anxious you, a less vigilant you, a less worried you, a more peaceful you, a calmer you? We'll use the word *relaxed* to stand for these various states and conditions. You want a coaching session to be a relaxed sort of thing, both for you and for your client, rather than a grind, an anxious affair, or something to dread. For it to be easygoing, you will need to bring the relaxation with you. How *you are* is how *the session will be*.

Vigilance is baked into us. But its intensity varies dramatically from situation to situation. When you're relaxed on your beach vacation, you may feel so calm and safe that you nod off without a worry. When, by contrast, you're interviewing for a job, appearing on television, driving just after having had an accident, or minding the grandkids, your arousal level is likely very high, and you will likely experience many of the symptoms we associate with anxiety. A sunny day at the beach and a job interview are different situations.

For many, if not most, coaches, coaching can feel more like a job interview than a sunny day at the beach. Indeed, you might suppose that coaching *ought* to feel more like a job interview than a sunny day at the beach. But there really isn't any "ought" involved here. Via practice and intention, you can experience a coaching session as an easygoing interlude. You can come in relaxed, stay relaxed, and end relaxed. Over time, via practice and intention and the confidence born of lots of coaching experiences, you can learn to coach calmly.

I am not supposing that you will be able to relax right away. But picture the difference between a young medical student performing her first surgery and a seasoned surgeon working carefully but calmly on her hundredth or thousandth surgery. It is not precisely that the seasoned surgeon is relaxed. But there is something of a practiced, confident, deep relaxation attached to what she does. She practices this not only for herself but to make her whole team calmer. You, too, can practice and learn this relaxed attitude, which will not only serve you but also serve your client.

EXERCISES

Easy. Say, "I intend to become a calm and relaxed coach."

Easy. Say, "Coaching can be like a day at the beach."

Medium. Visualize a relaxed coaching session. See it going easily and smoothly. No strain, no upsets, no tests, no upheavals. Just two people who are engaged, thoughtful, and occasionally even smiling.

High bar. We are talking about anxiety, and we are obliged to embrace the fact that we will never completely master or eradicate all of our anxiety. Therefore, it is smart to acquire one or two (or more) anxiety management tools that are both healthy and effective (that is, not Scotch or Valium). Do you possess a few of these? If you don't, you might want to spend the time and put in the effort required to learn some personal anxiety management strategies.

Food for Thought for Informal Coaches

Are you typically anxious when you interact with other people? Do you have mild or even moderate social anxiety? Is it time to work on that a little bit?

Writing Prompt for Self-Coaches

Write to the prompt "I would like to do some relaxed self-coaching. I think that would look like..."

6

You and Purpose

You may not have thought much about your philosophy of life or about how having or not having a philosophy of life might connect to your coaching. But it rather matters what you believe in, doesn't it? And it must be a good thing to know what it is you believe in, yes? To start with, what is it that you believe about the purpose of life?

If, for instance, you believe that life purpose is provided — as, say, a rabbi or a priest might be presumed to believe — then when a client is running short of purpose (which can manifest in all sorts of ways, from a lack of motivation to sleepless nights), you would logically respond, "Go with God." If you *really believed* that purpose came from on high, then you would naturally point your client there. If, however, you believed a very different thing, that we are obliged to choose our life purpose, then you wouldn't say, "Go with God." You would say, "You decide."

Of course, you could say nothing or simply return the matter to your client. But if you *really believe* that God provides purpose, can you say nothing? Or if you *really believe* that folks must take personal responsibility for their life purpose choices and not go hunting for purpose as if it were a lost wallet or misplaced car keys, can you say nothing? If you have convictions, mustn't that influence what you say and do?

It is one thing to affirm that your client is entitled to his or her opinions. That goes without saying. But if you believe that the road is washed out ahead, or that salmon left out for three days shouldn't be eaten, will you say nothing?

Yes, you could return the matter to your client by saying, "And how does that make you feel?" or "What are your thoughts about your lack of purpose?" or "Where do you think your problems with motivation come from?" Responses of this sort can produce results — up to a point. After a certain point, however, you must necessarily ratify or dispute your client's conclusion. If, say, your client throws up his hands and exclaims, "I think I'll wait for a sign from God!" and you believe in personal responsibility and not in gods, will you just nod? Maybe. Many coaches would. And that nod would certainly honor your client's right to decide. But is that the coach you want to be?

You may be thinking, "This is too hard. Let me just coach. I don't need to know any of this or think about any of this." Thinking that would certainly put you in the majority. But I'm inviting you to join a minority of people — and a minority of coaches — who actually try to fathom where they are coming from and who try to understand why they are suggesting what they are suggesting. Yes, you may have no real idea what you believe. But on what sort of footing would that put you? Is that a tenable position, to have no personal sense of what life is about? Wouldn't it be better if you knew?

Whatever your position is on your client's right to his or her opinions, I think you can see how *your* opinions must somehow also matter. How, exactly? Well, isn't that a good question to ponder? Let's spend some time today pondering that conundrum.

EXERCISES

Easy. Sit with the phrase "the purpose of life." Where does that take you?

Easy. Sit with the phrase "multiple life-purpose choices." Where does that take you?

Medium. What are your thoughts about the pros and cons of articulating one's philosophy of life?

High bar. Have you ever tried to articulate your philosophy of life? Want to give that a try today?

Food for Thought for Informal Coaches

Imagine that you are in a work environment, informally coaching your team members. Whose purpose do you have in mind? Your team members'? Yours? The company's? Reflect on the meaning of purpose when there are multiple agendas involved.

Writing Prompt for Self-Coaches

Write to the prompt "If I were to make the internal shift from the idea of the purpose of life to the idea of multiple life purposes, that would mean…"

7

You and Meaning

Golly, am I really asking you to think about that difficult, abstract, elusive thing called meaning? I am indeed. So much of coaching is ultimately about whether or not a client feels that his life is purposeful and meaningful. If these are core considerations, then a coach is rather obliged to know what she herself believes about purpose, as we discussed in the last chapter, and about meaning, the subject of this chapter.

It is actually surprisingly important that you understand your own views on meaning. Say that you're working as a life coach with a female client in her late thirties who brings up that she is wrestling with the question of whether or not to have children. She knows that she must address this question now, or very soon, or else she will have made her decision by default.

If, for instance, you believe that life has a particular meaning — that there is a meaning to life — you might consciously or inadvertently lobby for children, presuming that your client will lead a more meaningful life if she has children. If, however, you believe that everyone gets to make her own life-purpose choices, and that meaning might attach to any decision that she makes — to birth children, to adopt children, not to have children, et cetera — then you wouldn't feel any particular pull to overtly or subtly lobby for children.

Similarly, as a creativity coach, you might believe that it is more meaningful to create than not to create; or, on the other hand, you might believe that it is perfectly possible to live a life of meaningful experiences whether or not you create. Whichever belief system you hold to — that some things are clearly more meaningful than other things or that each person can make personal meaning in his or her own way — that belief system must influence what you see as the help you have to offer.

As you enter the world of coaching — or even if you've been coaching for some time already — it would be a good idea for you to pause and think through your relationship to meaning. If you feel, as I do, that meaning is a certain sort of subjective psychological experience and, as such, naturally comes and goes, you can help clients frame their current feelings of meaninglessness in a very different way from someone who has never thought through what he believes about meaning. If you do happen to feel as I do, then you can better help clients weather those naturally occurring dry spells of meaning than can someone who feels there is a meaning to life that must be found somewhere.

This is not an easy territory. But because so much of coaching is ultimately about meaning and purpose, it is a good idea for you to spend a little time — even if it is an uncomfortable time — coming to your own conclusions about the following two radically different positions: first, that there is a purpose to life or that it is truer to conceive of the possibility of multiple life-purpose choices; and, second, that there is a meaning to life or that it is truer to see meaning as a certain sort of subjective psychological experience that naturally comes and goes, one that is a renewable resource and a wellspring that clients can, with your help, coax into existence.

Of course, you might skip this examination. Most coaches — most human beings — do. But your coaching sessions will prove both deeper and more effortless if you have a settled personal sense of meaning and purpose. With the clarity that this settled sense would bring, you would do a better job of not pushing or pulling your clients in any particular direction. If you do this work, you will better understand your own motives and agendas — and that will prove a boon to clients.

Easy. Say, "I am willing to come to a personal understanding of meaning."

Easy. Sit with the phrase "Meaning is subjective." Notice how that feels and see what it conjures up for you.

Medium. What do the phrases "meaning investments" and "meaning opportunities" suggest to you? Do a little thinking and writing to this prompt.

High bar. If you would like to take some time out of your busy life to come to your own conclusions about meaning, create a little self-study plan for doing that.

Food for Thought for Informal Coaches

Imagine that you are informally coaching your child about an upcoming piano recital that he is dreading. Feel through how much better the coaching might go, and the recital, if you didn't pressure him to believe that this was going to be a meaningful experience but instead framed the event in some other way — as, say, an opportunity to share the music with a friendly audience. Can you feel that difference?

Writing Prompt for Self-Coaches

Write to the prompt "I'm surprised to realize that I found all of the following experiences meaningful..."

8

You and Possibility

A feature of your life philosophy is your position on possibility. What's possible, given human nature? What's possible in a given set of circumstances — say, if your client has a chronic illness or three small children at home? What's possible with respect to change and growth? And so on. You may be harboring some variation of the feeling that nothing much is possible for most people. Or, by contrast, you may feel that everything is possible, if you just believe. Or you may be someplace in between. To say this another way, are you a pessimist, an optimist, or some mix of the two?

The current mental disorder paradigm, where you acquire a mental disorder label for life, is a pessimistic paradigm. If, say, you are labeled a schizophrenic, well, then you will always be a schizophrenic. If you happen to be functioning well and not looking particularly schizophrenic, then your schizophrenia is said to be "in remission." You are still a schizophrenic — and always will be. The same is the case with ADHD, bipolar disorder, borderline personality disorder, et cetera. According to that pessimistic paradigm, you are a troubled lifer.

It is funny to say that the label "sadness" is a more optimistic take on mood than is "clinical depression," but it is. To say that someone is sad is to imply that the sadness might, and maybe even likely will, pass. But to say that someone is clinically depressed is to angle a person toward a lifetime of chemical responses to a putatively chronic condition. Most helpers nowadays are trained to go down that latter, pessimistic road.

You doubtless have thoughts and feelings about possibility, thoughts and feelings that you've probably never articulated. If, say, a client came to you with a history of never having been able to write the novel she has always wanted to write, what chance would you give her of writing that novel now? A 10 percent chance? A 40 percent chance? An 85 percent chance? Would you consider it highly unlikely or reasonably possible that she will be able to write her novel this time? What are your honest thoughts and feelings?

To my mind, it is good to be optimistic. That isn't to say that you should be foolhardy, naive, or unrealistic. But there is a very different energy between you and your client if you feel that she has a chance versus feeling that she really has no chance. Now, you may believe that the odds of her achieving her goals are long. But that's very different from secretly believing that her chances are nil. Say that your client is working on a screenplay. Yes, the odds of her selling it are long. But that is a very different sentiment from believing that she has no chance at all.

You may discover, if you investigate the matter, that many aspects of your personal philosophy are pretty pessimistic in nature. It would be lovely, and it would serve your clients a lot, if you could grow a bit more optimistic and hold that your clients have a chance: a chance to change, a chance to heal, a chance to succeed. It isn't that you need to put on rose-colored glasses or ignore or minimize reality. But your clients are more likely to *have a chance* if you hold that they have a chance.

EXERCISES

Easy. What are your first thoughts about possibility?

Easy. If you can, say, "I believe in possibility."

Medium. Do you believe that a client who has not been successful in the past can be successful in the future? If you believe that future success is possible for such a client, what might that future success depend upon?

High bar. Picture a hypothetical client with a history of trauma, difficult current circumstances, and substantial goals. Try holding the feeling that she has a chance to achieve her goals. From that place of optimism, how might your work with her proceed?

Food for Thought for Informal Coaches

Imagine coming to your informal coaching interactions with the feeling that things are possible rather than the feeling that things are difficult or that things are impossible. Can you feel how that change would brighten and lighten those interactions?

Writing Prompt for Self-Coaches

Write to the prompt "If I were to really feel that things are possible, then I would..."

9

You and Effort

Do you harbor beliefs that effort pays off, that luck is not just luck but is related to effort, that effects have causes, and other beliefs that together might be summarized as "Effort matters"? Or, maybe consciously or maybe only subconsciously, do you believe that you can get things done in some virtually effortless way, just by thinking them, wishing for them, or mastering some secret?

I believe in mystery, but I believe in effort more. At a counseling center where I once worked, a number of the counselors would spend a portion of their lunch hour praying for peace. I could not possibly have joined them, as I don't believe that peace is achieved by praying. I believe that you need an army larger than Hitler's to defeat a Hitler and a lot of effort put in by a great many men and women to wrest peace from the world's war makers. That is my belief system. What is yours?

Your client wants certain things. She has goals, dreams, ambitions, and plans; and she has challenges to overcome. Will you stand neutral on the matter of effort, as therapists are taught to do? The therapist is trained only to "diagnose" and "treat." In that model, the client becomes less depressed, say, because he is taking the right antidepressant rather than because he is getting out of his hateful job or his imploding marriage. For mental health professionals operating according to the mental disorder paradigm, the client is "treated," not invited to work. A pill does the trick — a magic trick, we might say.

Coaches, on the other hand, need their clients to make an effort. How strongly you push and how pointedly you focus on effort will depend in large measure on your own beliefs about effort. Do you consider yourself laid back and feel that, for instance, it's fine to write the book you're sort of writing only when you're feeling inspired? Or do you suppose that a book only gets written if its author makes an effort on days when he or she doesn't want to be writing? This fundamental, personal difference in belief — "I write only when I'm inspired" versus "I write every day" — must of course get reflected in how you coach, what you expect of clients, and what you ask of clients.

You can tell that I'm an advocate for effort. I believe in mystery, synchronicities, cosmic oddities, flashes of brilliance, and the fact that we do not know what we do not know. But we *do* know that for most things we need to get done or want to have happen, we had better work at them. We had better put in the effort, put in the hours, sweat, burn the midnight oil, and so on. Do you agree? And if you do, how will that belief play itself out in your coaching?

EXERCISES

Easy. Ponder the question "What are my beliefs about effort?"

Easy. Ponder the question "My beliefs aside, what are my actual lived experiences? Where have I made an effort, and where haven't I?"

Medium. Are you pretty good at making an effort, or do you have trouble making an effort? How do you think your personal relationship to making an effort might play out in your work with clients?

High bar. Let's say that you really wanted to make an effort of some sort, but you knew from your past history and experiences that X,

Y, and Z were going to stand in the way. How might you handle X this time? How might you handle Y? How might you handle Z? If one of these seems rather intractable, maybe because you believe it is a baked-in feature of your personality, can you envision handling it with some completely new tactic or some inventive work-around?

Food for Thought for Informal Coaches

How might you invite the folks you informally coach to make an effort without pressuring them, making demands on them, or nagging them? Can you picture how you might walk that line?

Writing Prompt for Self-Coaches

Write to the prompt "With respect to my number one self-coaching goal, I am going to make the following effort..."

10

You and Human Nature

If you were raising sheep, goats, and alpacas, you would want to know something about sheep, goats, and alpacas. You would want your knowledge to be empirical, based on the reality of sheep, goats, and alpacas, not theoretical, based on principles you posit from on high about all living things. If shearing a sheep was one sort of thing and shearing an alpaca was another sort of thing, you would want to know that.

As a coach, you want to know about human beings and their nature and appreciate that you can't override or ignore human nature. Ignoring or trying to override human nature sounds like saying, "Just say no to drugs" or "Just say no to sex." Oversimplifying or romanticizing human nature sounds like saying, "Everybody is basically good" or "Everything is for a purpose." Falsifying our experience of reality sounds like saying, "But that happened so long ago. Why aren't you over that by now?" Sheep have a reality and a nature, goats have a reality and a nature, alpacas have a reality and a nature, and human beings have a reality and a nature. We ought not to ignore that, oversimplify that, or falsify that.

Your clients will know, either consciously or just outside of conscious awareness, whether or not you have a decent understanding of human nature and whether or not you are operating from a truthful place with respect to human nature. If, for instance, you were to encourage a client to blow the whistle at work without inviting him to also consider the consequences, your client would understand that you had no idea about how real life operates; or, if you did, that you were ignoring your understanding for the sake of supporting some slogan-sized principle like "Always tell your truth."

Whether or not you have ever articulated a coherent or comprehensive philosophy of life for yourself and whether or not you have a full or complete understanding of human nature, you will experience coaching as a much richer and much more human enterprise, and so will your clients, if you come to sessions ready to talk about real, human things and not programmatic or superficial things. Prohibition didn't stop drinking — it produced bootleggers and speakeasies. *That* is human nature. Come to sessions raring to dive into human reality.

You need to know about and reckon with the reality of human beings if you want to work with human beings, just as you need to know about and reckon with the reality of sheep if you want to raise sheep for meat, milk, or wool. Raising sheep is not a romantic proposition. Neither is coaching human beings. In both cases there is a lot of muck, mire, and sheer reality. Let that be deeply okay.

You might want to create a new overarching or underlying principle for your work with human beings: "I am working with real people, in all their richness, darkness, and complexity." Do not expect the person sitting across from you to be "a client." He or she is a human being. You master the coaching session by opening up to that reality, that human beings are exactly who they are — and that one of our species is sitting across from you.

EXERCISES

Easy. Just be with the phrase "human nature." Feel it and be with it.

Easy. Say, "I accept the realities of human nature." Or find your own way of phrasing the idea that to coach means to deal with human beings.

Medium. Write to the prompt "I suspect that the following aspects of human nature are going to trouble me the most…"

High bar. Try your hand at distinguishing between personality and human nature.

Food for Thought for Informal Coaches

Do you have the sense that there are some basics about human nature? Have you ever stopped to articulate them?

Writing Prompt for Self-Coaches

Write to the prompt "Some of the following features of my nature feel learned or acquired, and some feel basic or original…"

11

Gathering Information Simply

B efore you meet with a new client, three things will likely happen. First, you will gather some information from your client, so that you can hit the coaching-session ground running. Second, you will sit with that information and begin to think of what might help and where help may *really* be needed. Third, you will feel through what sharing that information may have meant to your client and how vulnerable that may have made her. Today, let's look at the first of these: gathering some information.

It is good to know something about your client and his or her goals and challenges before you meet for the first time. This isn't a must — you could meet with a new client and simply say, "What's on your mind?" or some equivalent — but it is really a very good idea and helps you to deepen and ground the first session if you have some information beforehand. Knowing at least a little about your client before you meet is valuable.

You can do this very simply. Once a client session is scheduled, you can send your client an email, asking him or her to answer a few questions. In my own case, I send new creativity coaching clients the following email:

Hello,

Great to be working with you! If you would, I'd love it if you'd answer the following three questions to get me oriented.

1.   Can you start by describing your situation a little? What sort of art do you do, what's been your history with art making and art selling, what ups and downs have you experienced, and so on? Please write as little or as much as you like — but enough to give me a starting picture of where you're at and where you've been.

2.   What are your biggest challenges right now, either internal or external, with respect to your creative life?

3.   What would you like to accomplish over the next few months with respect to your creative life? Do you maybe have some minimum goals and also some "Wow, that would be great!" goals?

I look forward to getting your responses. Take as long as you like, but try not to labor too long over this <smile>. And, of course, add anything you think is relevant that these three questions don't get at.

Best,

Eric

P.S. If you would, please let me know that you received this email. Thanks!

This email typically gets me a lot of information, all the information I need to get started. Naturally, you will ask the questions you think sensible to ask. But my email might serve you as a pretty good model. It is not overwhelming, it is friendly, and it works well. Give my model some thought — and begin to think about yours.

EXERCISES

Easy. Feel which way you are leaning: toward gathering no information from a new client, toward gathering a little information, or toward gathering a lot of information?

Easy. Say, "No matter how much information I get or how troubling or intractable my client's problems seem, I will stay calm."

Medium. Feel through what you will do when the information arrives, especially if there is a lot of it. Will you panic? Will you internally exclaim, "This is too much!" Will you leap to some problem-solving place? Or, fingers crossed, will you remain deeply calm?

High bar. Craft your own information-gathering email. How can you get enough useful information without overwhelming your client with questions? See if you can walk that line between asking for too little and asking for too much. Don't worry about perfecting this email, as you won't really know if it works until you try it out on new clients, and you can adjust and refine it as you go along. Do the best you can for now and ready yourself to send it out when the time comes.

Food for Thought for Informal Coaches

Imagine that you're meeting tomorrow with one of the team members you manage and that you expect you'll need to do a little informal coaching. You could just wing it — or you could prepare by asking your team member some questions and gathering some information first. As you think about this situation, do you feel resistant to gathering that information? If so, why do you think you might be feeling resistant?

Writing Prompt for Self-Coaches

Part of the art of coaching yourself is gathering information from yourself. Try the following. Pick a current challenge that you're facing. It could be a health challenge, a work challenge, a relationship challenge, or anything else you'd like to work on. Rather than trying to solve it, write to the prompt "What information do I need from myself that would help me better understand this situation?" Try to feel the difference between solving problems and gathering information.

12

The Act of Sharing

When you ask your client for information prior to your first session together, you are asking her to reveal her private thoughts and feelings; you are asking her to share intimate details of her life, including embarrassing ones; and you are asking her to stand vulnerable before you. It is good to remember that this is what you are doing.

How would *you* feel telling another person that you can hardly find the motivation to get out of bed, or that none of your paintings sold at your last gallery show, or that you grew up with authoritarian parents, or that your career is stagnant and feels like it's on the way down? How would you feel revealing information of that sort?

This sharing can be a beautiful thing. But it sours almost instantly if, as a coach, you respond to it too matter-of-factly. You want to respond with humanity, not dryly. However, responding with humanity is not at all like responding with a smiley-face emoji, just to lighten the mood. The opposite of matter-of-fact is not cheerful. Try to acknowledge, first of all internally, how hard a time your client is having of it. The opposite of matter-of-fact might initially, in your mind, sound like, "Wow, that is a lot! To spend sixty hours a week at a draining day job and then to try to compose your musical — how hard! I'm amazed that you're getting to it at all!"

Your client is sharing that it is hard for her, and you want to hear her. It isn't that you need (or ought) to say a lot in response to the information that your client sends you before the first session. The actual reply you make may be as brief as "Thank you for this. We will have a lot to talk about when we meet." You don't have to wring your hands and commiserate. Just acknowledge in a human way that you have heard her, that you understand a lot is going on, and that, while you intend to be of help, there is likely no quick fix in the offing.

Think of how you would feel sharing your private life and, even more dramatically, your secret life. Would you want anyone to know about your lusts, your desires, your revenge fantasies, your guilty pleasures? That you were reprimanded at work, made some really bad investments, drink a bit more than you confess to? All of this you are innocently asking your client to divulge when you ask a question like "Tell me a little bit about what might get in the way of you reaching the goals you'd like to set?" What is that "little bit"? Nothing less than the part of her life she would rather not talk about.

EXERCISES

Easy. Say, "I understand that my client is making himself or herself vulnerable."

Easy. Say, "I am going to be both caring and careful."

Medium. Try your hand at revealing yourself to you. Write about one of those disappointments you don't like to talk about or an action you took that still makes you feel guilty. Get a sense of how your own defenses work and how sharing sensitive material feels.

High bar. Get a picture in your mind's eye of the long email a hypothetical client has sent you in reply to your request for information. Try crafting a reply that shows you have heard him. Experiment with a few different ways of responding until you hit on one that sounds authentic and most like your voice.

Food for Thought for Informal Coaches

In many settings, coaching can feel like criticism. Between the lines, you may be implying, "Look, you're having a problem with this. Let's get it corrected." Think about the extent to which a person might not want to share much in those circumstances. If *you* were being criticized, would you feel particularly safe or eager to open up? Given what amounts to very natural reticence in such situations, how might you make it easier for someone you were coaching to share?

Writing Prompt for Self-Coaches

Write to the prompt "Today I am going to reveal to myself one of the secrets I keep from myself. And I am going to be okay revealing it! Among the secrets I keep from myself is the following one…"

13

Conceptualizing Help

You are getting ready to be of help. This sounds so simple! But what does someone in need of help actually need? Well, if the problem is a leaking pipe, they need someone who can fix the leak. They would also like that person to come quickly, to charge a reasonable rate, to actually fix it and not just cosmetically fix it, and maybe to guarantee the work. We have a rather clear sense of what's needed when it comes to a plumber. We would like the plumber to be competent, honest, reliable, and perhaps pleasant — though pleasant may not be our highest priority.

But what about coaching? What help is our new client expecting or wanting? They may be able to say what is wrong — that they aren't practicing their music, that their boss at work is bullying them, that they can't find meaning in life, that they're frustrated by their lack of motivation or commitment, et cetera. But to announce what is wrong is not the same as identifying what's wanted or needed or what they are expecting from us. Life issues are not like plumbing issues; and coaching is not like consulting or psychotherapy.

Let's take as the presenting problem that your new client isn't writing their novel. A plumber might look for a hole in the novel's plot. And that might indeed be something that your client needs, to shore up their plot. Can you help with that? Yes and no. You aren't a plot doctor. But you can wonder aloud if that might be an issue. That is, a major component of the help you are offering is *putting things on the table.* And if your client happens to say, "Yes! That is a part of the problem!" then you get to say, "Great! And what would you like to try?" A second major component of the help you are offering is *aiming your client toward action.* Those two together are both what your client needs and what you are offering.

At the same time, you are being modest. Unlike a plumber, you are in no position to fix anything. No matter how bright your flashlight or how sturdy your wrench, you are not dealing with the equivalent of a plumbing problem. Too much is outside of your control; too much may be outside of your client's control as well. And, as the saying goes, it's complicated. Your client may say that they want to work on their novel, but they may have many reasons for not working on it, among them, for instance, that its theme embarrasses them by revealing too much about them. Well, that's a fine pickle! This is nothing like fixing a broken pipe.

So you are obliged to be modest and hold what you are doing as "helping a little." Yes, you may ultimately help a lot. And it is fine to hope that you may help a lot. But it is wise to come to that first session with very modest expectations — maybe only with the expectation that you will be able to get some useful things on the table and that, with your client's assistance, the two of you will be able to find some things for them to try.

We can combine these three ideas into a simple coaching mission statement: "I am going to try to get things on the table, aim my client in the direction of action, and be of some help." To do that is to do a lot!

EXERCISES

Easy. Say, "I can be of some help."

Easy. How might you get things on the table with a friend? Picture how that might go.

Medium. Get a clear picture in your mind of how a friend can help a friend. Contrast that with how a plumber fixes a leak. Try to get a good, solid, settled understanding of the difference between solving a problem and being of some help.

High bar. If an important coach's goal is to motivate clients to take action — well, what actually helps motivate a person to take action? What are your thoughts on this centrally important question?

Food for Thought for Informal Coaches

Picture a team member at work coming to you for some help. He describes the problem he is having, a problem with another team member. Get this situation clearly in mind. Now, think about how you would answer the following questions: Are you comfortable bringing them together, coaching them both at the same time, and helping them resolve their conflict? Is that a skill you have in your repertoire? If it isn't, might that be a useful skill to learn?

Writing Prompt for Self-Coaches

Write to the prompt "In my own life, I can get things on the table by..."

14

Musing and Wondering

Unlike a mental health helper — a psychiatrist, psychologist, psychotherapist, family therapist, et cetera — you are not burdened by the need to translate the information your client has provided into "symptom picture" language or "mental disorder" language. If she says that she had trouble adjusting to art school, you don't have to start thinking, "Adjustment disorder." If she says that she's demoralized by world events, you don't have to start thinking, "Clinical depression." You don't have to approach the information your client has shared with you with a checklist at your side.

What you can profitably do instead is simply muse and wonder. You can wonder what it might feel like if *you* had composed three symphonies that had never been played publicly and now you were trying to begin a fourth one. Would *you* feel very motivated? Wouldn't you in your heart of hearts wonder what the point was, given what must feel like zero prospects for your infant symphony? Aren't the odds substantial that you might not be able to face that fourth symphony at all? If those were your experiences, wouldn't they make doing a hard thing, composing a symphony, even harder?

Say that in response to your information-gathering email, your new life coaching client has provided you with the information that he wants to start a certain sort of home business. He is very eager to start ... and then you read in the next paragraph that he has three young children at home. Can you imagine being able to pay attention to a fledgling business with three small children scampering about? What seems possible or plausible in such circumstances? How would you game-plan that situation, if it were your life? Would you even be *able* to game-plan, given that the kids are exclaiming, "I'm starving!" every two minutes? Before you would dream of trying to solve your new client's problems, wouldn't you first want to picture his real world of laundry, kid squabbles, and exhaustion?

This isn't some sort of formal operation, with a checklist at your side or programmatic ideas in mind. You are just musing and wondering. You are wondering about your client's life, how his experiences may have affected him, what impact his current circumstances may be having on him, what it's like to be him. You're musing, not worrying or calculating. Yes, you may already have worries — that he feels difficult, that his goals are unrealistic, that his life is unmanageable — but you quiet those worries, give him the benefit of the doubt, and engage in the lightest of musing and wondering.

The coaching session is like this, too; and so is the time between sessions, especially if your client is checking in with you on his progress. Each check-in is an opportunity to muse and wonder. "Hmm, I wonder why that happened?" "Hmm, I wonder how he's feeling about not having managed to work on his business plan?" "Hmm, it looks like he's tripping in the same spot again. What might be useful to say? A little cheerleading? Or some pointed suggestion?" You do this musing lightly, as if you were a weightless spirit hovering in your client's world. You look, you see, you feel, you muse, you wonder.

In this chapter, we're still looking at that period of time before your first session with a new client. You haven't had a first session yet, so you *really* don't know this person. What you have is the information he's provided and your understanding of human nature. It is far too soon to draw any conclusions, especially any negative ones about how hard this will be. Just be with your client's information, relax, and feel privileged to be allowed into this fascinating world, the world of a living, breathing human being. Relax there; wander there; and let yourself wonder.

Easy. Say, "I don't have to leap to problem-solving. I can begin by just musing and wondering."

Easy. Pick something to muse about. See if you can muse.

Medium. Picture in your mind's eye the great many paragraphs of information that your client has provided. Feel into how to be with this wealth and mass of information lightly, rather than anxiously.

High bar. Go to some therapist's, coach's, writer's, or artist's website on the internet. Find their "About Me" page and muse about their life. What feels like it hasn't gotten said? What hunches are percolating up in you? What questions might you like to ask to elicit more information? Be with this stranger's "About Me" page and do a little musing and wondering.

Food for Thought for Informal Coaches

In life, and especially in our fast-paced contemporary life, it is very hard to just muse and wonder. Say that a coaching opportunity appears on the horizon. Can you picture yourself carving out some time and space to muse and wonder before your meeting? What might it look like to create that opportunity, that time, and that space?

Writing Prompt for Self-Coaches

Self-coaching is the tool; self-awareness is the goal. We gain self-awareness by taking a step to the side of life to muse and wonder about our situation. Write to the prompt "I am giving myself time and space to just muse and wonder about..."

15

Game-Planning

A football coach's game plan can be very elaborate, with notes for players at every position and detailed strategies for predictable situations. He can even decide which dozen plays his team will run first, independent of the defense thrown at the team. His plan can be that strict, detailed, and elaborate. Or his plan can sound as simple as "Our opponent on Sunday is very weak against the run, so we are going to run the ball *a lot*."

If it seems valuable to you to create a game plan for your upcoming first session, it almost certainly ought to be of that second sort. It must necessarily and naturally be extremely short. You might come to that first session with maybe three or four ideas in mind, but you surely wouldn't think of arriving with anything like a detailed playbook at the ready.

Your minimal plan might sound like: "I want to make sure to check in on the fact that she has no dedicated work space for her art, wonder aloud why she is only looking for local galleries to represent her, and get a better sense of why she wants to leave a day job that sounds pretty decent."

Or it might sound like: "I think a major goal will likely be to help him choose among the three ideas he has for a genealogical research project and help him tentatively commit to one of them. Then we can go on to setting up a daily practice in the service of that goal."

Or it might sound like: "My new client says that they currently spend sixty hours a week at work and can't understand why they can't find time to practice with their band and do everything else in life. There's a lot to unpack here. First, I think, is to wonder if they really *need* to be spending sixty hours at work — or if something else might be going on."

You do not need to have any game plan at all in place, except, as we discussed in the last chapter, the plan to get things on the table, point your client in the direction of action, and try to be of some help. If, however, you feel the pull to come armed with some plan, you will want it to be short and sweet, so that you can remember it and so that it allows real spaciousness for your client to go where he or she needs to go during the session.

A football coach's *essential* game plan never really varies. It's pretty much "Let's play to our strengths and exploit the other team's weaknesses." As simple as this is to say and as simple as this is to remember, it's fascinating how often even a seasoned coach will forget this basic game plan and thereby reduce his chances of success. Likewise, a life coach has a simple, essential game plan — to get things on the table, to point his client in the direction of action, and to be of some help — that he, too, may forget. Whatever other game plan you might create for a given client or session, if you remember this prime directive, you're unlikely to go very wrong.

EXERCISES

Easy. Say, "Short and sweet game-planning is easy."

Easy. Say, "If I think I need a game plan, I can easily create one."

Medium. Think through the extent to which you feel that you do or don't need to come to a session with a game plan in mind or in hand.

High bar. Create several hypothetical clients, imagine their challenges and their circumstances, and try to minimally game-plan for a first session with each of those hypothetical clients.

Food for Thought for Informal Coaches

What sorts of simple game plans make sense for you to create, given the sort of coaching that you find yourself sometimes doing?

Writing Prompt for Self-Coaches

You're coaching yourself on a particular issue. You have a certain goal in mind. Write to the prompt "Given the goal I have in mind, here is my plan..."

16

Smile

Your client arrives, let's say via computer video. You let her onto
the platform, and she appears on-screen. What do you do first?
Smile.

This is not trivial. This is not cosmetic. Rather, this is you
warming up the moment. Your smile doesn't have to be radiant, but
it is like a radiator. It warms the space and lets your client sigh into
the space.

If you come in anxious and fidgety, fussing with the controls
or nervous about the sound level, your client will remain in the
agitated state in which she, too, has arrived. The setup will then be
one of nervous energy for both of you. But if the first thing she sees
is you smiling...ah, that has such a calming effect!

Why might you not be able to smile?

- Maybe because you have something on your mind. The
  answer? Clear your mind before you open the video app.
  Exhale. Let everything go. Now, smile.
- Maybe because you anticipate a difficult session. The answer? Predict that the session will go well. Visualize ease.
  Let go of the natural tension that comes with having to deal
  with another human being. Breathe.
- Maybe because you can't quite remember who this client
  is or what the two of you are supposed to be working on.

The answer? Keep simple notes that help you identify and remember clients. A given note might be as brief as "North Carolina, working on a science fiction screenplay set on Mars, mom recently passed away, issues of self-confidence, organization, and motivation."

- Maybe because you fear not knowing what to do or what your client may throw at you. The answer? Deeply embrace that not knowing is okay. Don't just pay lip service to that central truth: feel how true it *is*. Would somebody sitting across from you know what's inside you or what you need, just like that, merely by virtue of sitting down and facing you? Impossible. You wouldn't expect him or her to know. Give yourself that same permission not to know.

These several preparations might take you no more than a minute or two. You clear your mind, glance at your notes to remember who this client is, predict ease, open to all that you do not know and can't know (but can inquire about), and get ready to smile. If you regularly and routinely engage in these simple preparations, you will have created a complete preparation routine that will allow you to begin each session with a smile. And if you arrive smiling, that will warm your client, likely cause her to smile, too, and instantly deepen the session.

There is no demand that you smile *during* the session, as during the session you may be dealing with serious matters. A session need not be and may not be some sort of smiling affair. But that first smile...well, that's welcome, welcoming, and important!

EXERCISES

Easy. Complete the prompt "I think I may have some trouble starting sessions with a smile because..."

Easy. The next time you see someone, try smiling. See if you can.

Medium. Picture an upcoming session that you are really not looking forward to. Create that scenario in your mind, maybe picturing a difficult client, a hard issue, or both. Now, see yourself smiling as the session begins. Did that initial smile change your feelings about the session or change the tone of the session?

High bar. Create your own preparation routine. Identify the different obstacles to smiling that might challenge you, from fatigue to fear of the encounter, from doubts about your competence to your current distractibility. For each one, create a simple answer that you include in your personal preparation routine.

Food for Thought for Informal Coaches

Imagine informally coaching your child. Would you be stern, or might you be able to smile?

Writing Prompt for Self-Coaches

Write to the prompt "I have many goals, dreams, ambitions, and intentions. When I think about them, I never smile. If I could smile as I thought about them, maybe..."

17

The First Thing You Say

You've smiled. What's the first thing to say? Maybe: "Good to see you!" Now you inquire from the heart, "How are you?"

Many professionals do not have to greet you from the heart. Your plumber, accountant, lawyer, or doctor may need to provide only a perfunctory greeting — you don't need much more from him or her. But as a coach, you are in a different category.

You aren't a high-on-a-pedestal expert. You aren't here to fix a problem. You have come to meet another person where he or she is most human, most vulnerable, most troubled, and most in need of support. Coming from the heart is a real, energetic manifestation of the support you intend to offer. So you smile and say, "Good to see you! How are you?"

Of course, you might say something different. Maybe "How are you?" sounds perfunctory or off base to you. Maybe you'd prefer, "Good to see you! I'm very much looking forward to working with you!" Or "Good to see you! I wonder, do you have a place you'd like to start?" Or, as a little icebreaker, and as this may be a Zoom call with no sense of place, "Good to see you! Where are you calling in from?"

In each case, the intention is the same. You are opening with a smile, enthusiasm, and the announcement that you are here and you are ready. It has that combination feel of rolling up your sleeves and giving a warm handshake. You are saying, "Good to be here!"

and "Let's do this!" Of course, it may be the case that in a matter of minutes or even in a matter of seconds, the two of you will grow somber as the work unfolds. But in those first few seconds, before the work actually begins, you get to set the tone by opening cheerfully, optimistically, and energetically.

It may not work so well to begin with, "Where would you like to start?" Your client has a lot on her mind and likely has many issues and challenges facing her, and that way of beginning demands that she arrive at a clear starting place. Although it amounts to the same question, it is rather better to say, "Did you have a starting place in mind?" By asking the question this way, you subtly acknowledge that your client may *not* know where to start — and that that's okay.

It may be even better to say something like, "Great to begin! You mentioned many things in the email that you sent me. Does one stand out as the place to start?" This does an even better job of acknowledging and honoring that a lot is going on for her and that she may not know which issue to choose to present.

Of course, you can also suggest a starting place. This might sound like, "Good to see you! Great to be working with you! You know, you identified several challenges in the email you sent me. I thought we might start with the restaurant you're trying to launch. Does that sound like a good starting place?" To this, your client will likely nod or shake her head — and if she shakes her head, that means that she has a place where she would prefer to start, which is good news.

In this way, you begin. It is easy, effortless really, and human sized. Isn't that a good place for two humans to begin?

EXERCISES

Easy. Say, "Good to see you!" How does that feel?

Easy. Say, "How are you?" How does that sound to you? Anything off about it? Is there something different you'd prefer to say?

Medium. Picture how two friends meet. What do they say to each other first? How do human beings greet each other?

High bar. Picture beginning. You've opened your Zoom window, and you're waiting for your client to arrive. Her name pops up in the waiting room. As you let her in, picture yourself growing easy. Enjoy this first meeting. And when she appears, smile. Then say the first thing that you intend to say. Picture that sequence.

Food for Thought for Informal Coaches

How do you greet people? Gruffly? With closed lips? Cheerfully? Are you playing a role at such moments? What is that role?

Writing Prompt for Self-Coaches

Write to the prompt "Each new day, I tend to greet myself in the following way..."

18

The Second Thing You Say

You begin by saying, "Good to see you! How are you?" or your version of a cheerful, enthusiastic, energetic greeting. And the second thing you say? The second thing you say depends on how your client replies to your opening question.

Let's look at three simple first session scenarios.

Scenario 1

You: "Good to see you! How are you?"
Client: "I'm okay. And I'm glad to be working with you."
You: "Great! Did you have a starting place? What's on your mind?"
Client: "It's my kickboxing practice! I'm not doing it."
You: "Okay! Tell me more about that."

And then you listen, inquire, advise, and all the rest...

Scenario 2

You: "Good to see you! How are you?"
Client: "I'm pretty miserable. I've been having a really hard time."
You: "Ah, I'm really sorry to hear that. Tell me what's been going on."

Scenario 3

You: "Good to see you! How are you?"

Client: "I could be better. And I doubt that you can help me."

You: "Well, let's see if I can be of some help. Let's begin with you telling me a little bit about what's going on."

This is how a first session might begin. The procedure is similar for ongoing sessions, as in the following examples.

Scenario 4

You: "Good to see you! How has the week been?"

Client: "It's been pretty rocky. I didn't manage to do any of things we agreed I'd do."

You: "Ah, that's too bad. Tell me about that."

Scenario 5

You: "Good to see you! How has the month been?"

Client: "Terrific! I've had a great month."

You: "Wonderful! Tell me more!"

Scenario 6

You: "Good to see you! How have things been going since we last met?"

Client: "Very mixed. I haven't managed to exercise or to diet. But I did manage to write for twenty minutes almost every day."

You: "Okay! Where should we start? With the exercise and the diet? Or with the poetry?"

The first thing you say is the equivalent of a hearty greeting. The second thing you say is the equivalent of a request, some version of "Tell me more." This greeting, followed by this request, is the way that sessions can typically — and effectively — start. It can all be kept this simple, as simple as opening a door. You step into your client's world, say hello, inquire as to how things are going, and begin.

You may think that there is something fancier, more conceptual, or more professional to do. But, in fact, helping almost always begins with a greeting and a "Tell me what's going on" invitation. To be sure, that "Tell me" might aim a client in a certain direction, as when a classical Freudian analyst or Jungian depth psychologist asks, "What have you been dreaming about?"

That is your choice, too. Your initial "Tell me" can either invite your client to pick a direction, as a response to your "Tell me what's been going on," or it can direct a client to go in a certain direction, as a response to your "Tell me how the novel has been going" or "I wonder, did you have that conversation you intended to have with your husband?" Whether with an open-ended question or with a directive question, you are inviting your client to check in and tell you more. That is a useful and effective second thing for you to do.

EXERCISES

Easy. Practice saying, "Tell me about that."

Easy. Practice saying, "Can you tell me more about that?"

Medium. What do you see as the pros and cons of this "Tell me about that" approach?

High bar. Create a few simple scenarios of the sort I created above and see what sort of language you might use to invite your client to tell you more. Try out a lot of different client issues and presentations, so as to gain some practice in saying, "Tell me more" in a variety of situations.

Food for Thought for Informal Coaches

Maybe you find asking for more information from someone you're informally coaching to be a bit pushy, rude, or intrusive. Picture trying to help a friend. See if you can get over your disinclination to ask for more information. In your mind's eye, picture yourself saying, "Tell me a little more about that."

Writing Prompt for Self-Coaches

Pick one of your self-coaching projects. Write to the prompt "Let me tell myself a little more about what's going on here..."

19

The First Few Minutes

During the first few minutes of a session, after you've said your second thing and your client has replied, you are doing two things at once: (1) You are listening, being present, and interacting. (2) You are also *assessing* whether or not you are in the right place. This is a very interesting, intricate, but also completely masterable way of being.

Imagine that you are chatting with your ten-year-old about a homework assignment of his. You are listening, being present, and interacting. But you might also be thinking, "Wow, this homework is far too easy for him. No wonder he's having trouble getting it done!" This thought, which you know is a really important thought and whose answer may hold the key to how well or how poorly fifth grade goes, now distracts you — and well it should. It is that important, and being distracted is a natural consequence of assessing.

What might you do?

- You might announce your observation. This might sound like, "You know, it looks like this is easy for you," and you then wait to hear what your son has to say.
- You might announce your observation and add a question. This might sound like, "You know, it looks like this is easy for you. Is everything at school easy for you?"
- You might announce your observation, add a question, and

express a concern. This might sound like, "You know, it looks like this is easy for you. Is everything at school easy for you? And if everything *is*, is that a problem?"

- You might announce your observation, add a question, express a concern, and make a recommendation. This might sound like, "You know, it looks like this is easy for you. Is everything at school easy for you? And if everything *is*, is that a problem? I wonder, should we think about finding some enrichment activities for you?"

Let's return to your work in session. The first few minutes you spend with a client are meant to give your client the space and time she needs to say what she needs to say. You are not rushing her, not leaning forward to leap in with a suggestion or a solution, not growing itchy to do something or say something. Instead, you are assessing and appraising.

And if and when the time comes, as it likely will, that you have the feeling you ought to interrupt your client's narrative so as to clarify a point, stick a stake in some fertile ground, or wonder aloud if the two of you might profitably go this way or that way, then trust your instinct. To ignore your own best sense of what feels needed next is to act too meekly in the moment. You will naturally and honorably give your client all the space and time she needs. But when it is *your* time, then you should bravely speak.

To say this another way, the first few minutes of a session — and the whole session, really — are a balancing act between following and leading. Your client has her part to play, but she is not talking to a vacuum tube. She gets to present, fully and with feeling; and you get to reply, likewise with feeling. This is the essence of the two of you being in it together.

EXERCISES

Easy. Picture yourself being easy with just listening.

Easy. Picture yourself being equally easy with jumping in.

Medium. Picture yourself doing both: deeply and calmly listening and actively and energetically jumping in. Can you feel how you can move back and forth between the two states or modes throughout a session?

High bar. Write a hypothetical client narrative — the story a client might present to you after you ask him to tell you more — and see if you can identify spots where you might profitably jump in. If you do this exercise and enjoy it, repeat it, as you will learn a lot that way.

Food for Thought for Informal Coaches

Your child is having a problem. You're trying to figure out what's going on. See if you can feel the difference between interrogating your child and gently jumping in so as to learn more.

Writing Prompt for Self-Coaches

Write to the prompt "I think that if, the next time I tell myself one of my usual stories, I were to jump in and ask myself what's really going on, I would discover..."

20

The Last Few Minutes

We'll look at the middle of sessions further on. Here, let's leap ahead to the end of the first session.

You and your client have agreed to be together for a certain amount of time, let's say forty-five minutes. As the session proceeds, the end starts to approach. The end of a session is typically experienced in one of three ways: (1) The session has started to drag a bit, and it feels a little like pulling teeth to get to the end. (2) It is hard to end the session, because so much is going on and because there is so much more to do. (3) Or, blissfully, you end exactly on time, with both of you experiencing a lovely sense of closure.

As we've seen, beginning a session is as easy as saying, "Good to see you!" Ending a session is harder. First, you are trying to hit a certain mark, say a quarter before the next hour. You may not only *want* to hit this mark but may *need* to hit this mark, as other timed tasks, like a next session, may be looming. Second, you want your client to know *exactly* what she is going to try to get accomplished between this first session and the second session. Third, you want to end on an up note, rather than a down note, and with a shared sense of hope and possibility. This is a lot … and naturally takes a bit of practice to manage.

With practice, you will learn how to do this effectively without thinking about it very much. You will be aware that a session is coming to a close and that you need both to summarize, so that your client knows exactly what's up, and also to aim for a hopeful, positive conclusion to the session. You do all this by taking charge of the last couple of minutes of the session and by saying something like the following: "Sorry to interrupt! We do have so much more to look at! But we're getting near the end of the session, and I want to make sure that I'm clear on what you're hoping to get done over the next two weeks. Can we focus there for a moment?"

"Yes."

"Great! That's excellent! Then let me do a bit of summarizing…"

If, after summarizing and engaging in a little cheerleading, you have arrived at your exact ending time, then you are done. If, however, there are still a few minutes remaining, you can either say, "I think that's a great place to stop!" and not worry about ending a few minutes early; or you can say, "Great! It looks like we have a minute or two remaining. Any last thing we should consider?" Typically, your client will reply, "No, I think that's a great place to end" — and you are done.

I always build into this summary the reminder that I am available for check-ins, if my client would like to check in regularly or periodically between sessions via email. I do not find these check-ins burdensome to handle, and I don't charge extra for them, but another coach might. This is a matter for each coach to decide, whether to allow for check-ins (and even lobby for them) or to skip offering them.

Ending a coaching session is a bit of an art form, but it is a process made up of understandable parts, including, from my point of view, the coach summarizing and the coach ending with hope. How might you end your first session?

EXERCISES

Easy. Say, "I can end sessions well."

Easy. Feel how a session might conclude easily and even effortlessly.

Medium. You are in the middle of a jam-packed interaction with your new client, and you also sense that you must wind the session down. What will you do?

High bar. List what you see as the tasks associated with ending a session. Then see if you can translate that list into a personal way of ending sessions.

Food for Thought for Informal Coaches

You have only a few minutes left before you must rush off to a meeting, and you're right in the middle of it with the person you're informally coaching. Picture yourself ending your time together well, despite all that pressure to finish up quickly. What does that look like?

Writing Prompt for Self-Coaches

Write to the prompt "I would end whatever I'm doing in a better way if I could mindfully remember to..."

21

Setting Up the Interval

The amount of time that passes between your first session and your second session depends on your setup. Will you meet with clients once a week, once every two weeks, once a month, or less frequently? The choice is yours.

What might help you decide on the interval you'd like to adopt? Here are a dozen considerations:

- More frequent sessions equal greater income.
- More frequent sessions equal less time for other things.
- More frequent sessions equal more fatigue (if they tire you).
- A short interval gives your client only a little time to get things done.
- A short interval also gives your client less time not to get things done.
- A longer interval gives your client more time to get things done.
- A longer interval also gives your client more time not to get things done.
- A long interval may lead to you and your client losing touch (unless you have a solid check-in protocol in place).
- The length of sessions needs factoring in. If the interval is short, short sessions might work well; if the interval is longer, longer sessions might make more sense.

- Your clients' needs and desires need factoring in.
- The time you have available needs factoring in.
- The energy you have available needs factoring in.

You may want the additional income that weekly sessions would garner, but you may only have the time and energy to meet with clients monthly. You may like the idea of short sessions (say, of half-an-hour duration) and also like the idea of meeting monthly with clients, but worry (probably rightly) that half an hour of contact once a month is just too little contact. In short, there may not be any perfect setup available to you. In that case, you will simply have to make your choices, put them into practice, and see how they work.

Personally, I meet with clients once a month for forty-five minutes. This works for me because my clients tend to check in with me regularly, meaning that we don't lose touch between sessions. I meet with clients only once a month in part because I think that is the right interval, but also because if I met with them more frequently, I wouldn't have time to do the other things that are also important to me. To accommodate my sixty clients, I currently set aside a dozen client days a month, five sessions a day. It's easy to do the math: if I were to meet with sixty clients more frequently than once a month, most of my time would be taken up with coaching.

Historically, psychoanalysts in the Freudian tradition met with clients four or five times a week. Imagine that! By contrast, an accountant or an estate attorney might meet with her clients once or twice a year. Then there is the hybrid model of regular appointments coupled with as-needed appointments. Think dentist: you have your two semiannual teeth cleanings and that emergency session when your tooth starts throbbing. All sorts of models exist, and each has its rationale. Likewise, you get to create your own model, according to what you think makes the most sense.

Whatever initial choice you make, you can change that setup over time, increasing or decreasing your intervals between sessions, increasing or decreasing the length of your sessions, et cetera. But to begin with, you will need to make a choice. What will your setup be?

Easy. Do you have a strong intuition about how often you'd like to see clients?

Easy. Do you have a single main consideration as to how often you'd like to see clients? Maybe it's income, fatigue factor, life balance, or…?

Medium. Visit the websites of some (or many) coaches and see how they set up their intervals. Muse on what you learn and/or what comes up for you.

High bar. Think through the pros and cons of the three most popular meeting intervals: meeting with clients once a week, meeting with clients every two weeks, and meeting with clients once a month. See what that analysis nets you.

Food for Thought for Informal Coaches

Imagine that you are monitoring something in your child's life — say, how well or how poorly he's doing in his algebra class. How often do you think you might like to check in with him about how it's going? What feels like intrusively too often, and what feels like too infrequently?

Writing Prompt for Self-Coaches

Let's say that you are monitoring something that's important to you, like your process of sending out your poetry manuscript to publishers. Write to the prompt "I think that I can best keep track of my submissions by…"

22

Where Is Your Client?

Your client may live in Boise, Boston, or Barcelona. That's where she will be during the interval between her first session and her second session. But where will she be in your life?

Will she be on your mind? Will you be thinking about her, worrying about her, or planning what you'll say to her the next time you see her? Or will you not be thinking about her at all between sessions?

Before you answer, imagine that you had twenty or thirty or forty clients. Where would *they* be? Could they *all* occupy a place in your thoughts? Does that seem plausible... or desirable?

If you have just one client, it's natural that you might think about her a lot. But if you had forty clients... well, that would demand a different approach, wouldn't it? What might that approach be?

I think a good approach is to remember that many things are important to you — that you have multiple life purposes — and that in order to attend to those several important things, you are obliged to organize the parts of your life carefully, including what you think about.

If you are mentally playing over something you said in session that you wish you hadn't said, then you aren't also playing a game with your child in a present way, or working on the nonfiction book you intend to write, or engaged in supporting a cause close to your heart, or having a quiet conversation with your mate — or doing nothing at all, for that matter. Thinking about what you said and being upset about what you said are *costs*. They cost you the chance to fully live your life purposes.

Let sessions go. Let things you might have said but didn't say go. Let things you did say and wish you hadn't said go. Let pestering preparations for upcoming sessions go. In short, let the coaching go and let clients go between sessions. Of course, you would be present for a client when and if she sends a check-in email and you need to reply to it. But otherwise free yourself from the burden of carrying clients around between sessions. Put that load down.

The answer to the question "Where is your client between sessions?" is that she is living her life. And you are living yours. Don't hold on to clients between sessions as a way of not living your life. It can be easier to pester yourself about a past or future client interaction than to face the fact that your relationship with your partner, building your coaching practice, cleaning up your home environment, attending to your health, or changing your lifestyle needs your attention. Let clients go between sessions, so that you can pay good attention to *your* life.

EXERCISES

Easy. Say, "I can let go of clients between sessions."

Easy. Visualize yourself free of clients between sessions. Enjoy that feeling.

Medium. Consider the many reasons why you might continue thinking about your clients between sessions: core worries and anxiety, a fear of doing too little or overlooking something, a way of avoiding the hard work of creating the class you intend to create or writing the play you intend to write. Get these reasons on the table and air them out.

High bar. Picture a hypothetical client with whom you are having a bit of a hard time, maybe because they are testing you, making subtle accusations about the quality or value of the coaching, always asking for more, or changing directions so often that you have no idea where you're at with them. Get that client clearly in mind — and now picture *not thinking about them* between sessions. See if you can do that and notice how that feels.

Food for Thought for Informal Coaches

Let's say that you are informally coaching someone in a rather irregular and impromptu way. How will you keep track of what's going on if your interactions are impromptu and irregular?

Writing Prompt for Self-Coaches

Write to the prompt "I don't want to pester myself about my self-coaching efforts, and I also don't want to forget about them. I think that I can create a balance that looks like the following…"

23

The Art of the Check-In

I invite all of my clients to check in with me via email on a regular and even a daily basis, as an aid in helping them stick to their intentions and as a way for them to hold themselves accountable.

I tell them that they are free to write as much as they like and that, most often, I'll reply with just a few words, like "Great!" or "Thanks for checking in," unless the check-in email requires more from me than that. I end every first session with a new client with the invitation to think about checking in with me between sessions.

Whether or not you invite clients to check in with you is completely up to you. It isn't any sort of "should." If you have the strong feeling that you would find such check-ins burdensome, time-consuming, and/or annoying, you might well not make such an offer. On the other hand, it might be good not to presume that you would find such check-ins burdensome or annoying and instead to give them a try. If they don't work for you, you need not offer them to future clients. But it might be a lovely thing to try out a few times, just to see how it works and how it feels.

A complete check-in exchange might sound like the following.

Client: "I got to my writing today, but only for twenty minutes, not for the full thirty minutes."
You: "Congrats on those twenty minutes! ☺"

In a nutshell, your objectives are to witness your client's efforts, cheerlead and celebrate, and, when and as appropriate, coach a little. The latter might sound like this.

Client: "I can't tell whether it would be better to just supply the information or create little stories. Readers of nonfiction seem to like those little stories!"

You: "Well, you might try writing a few paragraphs in each style, to see which seems to work better. Might that be an approach?"

I am comfortable making suggestions of this sort. You may not feel comfortable with such a tactic. You might nevertheless want to give it a try, to see how it works for you and also because it gives you practice in thoughtful suggesting. In session, you must make suggestions on the fly, which can feel pushy and make you anxious. By practicing suggesting in your email responses to client check-ins, you will hone your suggestion-offering skills. This might constitute another good reason to give check-ins a try.

Most clients will not want to check in with you daily or very regularly. If I ask a client how often she would like to check in with me, she will most likely say, "Maybe weekly?" My response would then be, "Great! Let's do that. What day of the week would you like that to be?" And, because it feels natural and customary, she will likely say, "Maybe Friday?" Typically, I would take this moment as an opportunity to summarize: "Okay, so for the next month you'll be working on A, B, and C, and you'll check in with me each Friday. Does that sound about right?"

This is a very brief look at what I think is a beautiful thing and a valuable tool in a coach's arsenal, the client check-in. In my experience, some clients will indeed write a lot, and a few will abuse the privilege and overdo their check-ins. But in general, clients are very mindful of your time and of the unspoken boundaries of this sort of interaction. You might want to take the risk and give this between-session add-on a try.

Easy. What are your first thoughts about offering your clients the opportunity to check in with you between sessions?

Easy. What feelings arise in you as you think about offering your clients the opportunity to check in with you between sessions?

Medium. Imagine that you were being coached. Would you like the opportunity to check in with your coach on your progress? Do you think that you would actually make use of that opportunity?

High bar. Craft a little speech announcing to clients that you are offering them the option of checking in with you between sessions. See if you can make it sound cheerful and generous but also possessing boundaries, so that it is clear what you are offering...and what you are not offering.

Food for Thought for Informal Coaches

How might you apply the idea of check-ins to your informal coaching?

Writing Prompt for Self-Coaches

Write to the prompt "I will check in with myself about my coaching goals and efforts by..."

24

Monitoring Homework, Goals, and Progress

Say that your client wants to do graduate work in archaeology at an Italian university. That's his goal. What homework might he assign himself that would help him meet that goal?

All of the following seem reasonable: that he learn about visa requirements, and student visa requirements particularly; that he learn about the difference in costs between Italian public and private universities; that he learn which Italian universities have archaeology departments and which of those archaeology departments are the highest rated; that he learn what the entrance requirements would be for the universities or university that he sets his heart and sights on; that he improve his Italian; et cetera.

A goal may be simple to articulate: "I want to do graduate work in archaeology at an Italian university." But achieving a goal of this sort is a great deal of work. It requires steady, focused attention and application, involves dealing with countless details, and calls for a level of organization that most clients are not accustomed to. To help your client reach this easy to say but hard to accomplish goal, you would profitably cocreate homework for him to do — and then monitor his efforts.

This might sound like you asking, "Okay, what are three things you might do this week in support of your goal?" Your client will likely have no great trouble naming three tasks: say, researching visa requirements, learning which Italian universities have archaeology departments, and getting a first sense of the costs involved. If you don't mind clients checking in with you, to this you might reply, "Great! Then why don't you check in with me on Friday and let me know what you've learned. How does that sound?" To this, your client might agree; or he might negotiate the time interval by saying, "You know, this is a superbusy week. Let me report to you in two weeks instead." To which you would reply, "Okay" — and the two of you would have an agreement in place.

When and if he does check in with you, you will not at all be surprised to learn that the homework was much harder to complete than your client expected it would be. He might exclaim, "Everything was in Italian!" or "The visa requirements are impossible to understand!" or "I couldn't make any sense of the costs!" You would be ready for this, because you understand reality and could have predicted these sorts of difficulties. So you might reply, "Yes, this is going to be a ton of work, isn't it? Let's go slowly and figure out our next steps."

Typically, the first homework assignment is ambitious and the second one more modest. You and your client might decide that he will next work on understanding the visa process, or determining which Italian universities have the best archaeology departments, or figuring out the costs, but not all three. He may have approached that first homework assignment with some enthusiasm. He may approach this one, even though it is reduced in scope, with a feeling of resignation, now that he understands the work and the difficulties involved. You would expect this shift from enthusiasm to resignation, and you would stand ready to cheerlead.

EXERCISES

Easy. Say, "I'm comfortable with the idea of giving clients homework."

Easy. Check in with yourself to see if you *are* comfortable with the idea of giving clients homework. If you aren't, do you perhaps want to change your mind about that?

Medium. Picture yourself working with a client over a significant period of time, during which the two of you cocreate homework assignments and monitor the client's progress. What does that look like? How does that feel?

High bar. Set yourself a significant homework assignment and see what it feels like to have that homework assignment looming over you. See if you procrastinate, get frustrated, go down unproductive rabbit holes, get only a tiny bit of the homework accomplished, and so on. These are the same sorts of experiences that your clients will have.

Food for Thought for Informal Coaches

How might you apply the idea of assigning homework to your informal coaching?

Writing Prompt for Self-Coaches

Write to the prompt "I think I will hold the idea of assigning homework in the following way..."

25

Coaching between Sessions

You may formally coach between sessions via email as part of your model and your practice. You may sometimes coach between sessions because of the nature of your relationship with a given client or because of the nature of the circumstances. Or you may shy away from coaching between sessions, maybe restricting your interactions to check-ins or maybe to no interactions at all. There is no right or wrong here — all of this is for you to choose.

I tend to sometimes coach between sessions. This typically happens when, for instance, a client has questions about the project she is working on and it makes sense to maintain a dialogue about that project via email. Or it might be that something has suddenly come up — say, a writer client learns that a literary agent would like to chat with her about representing her memoir — and it makes sense to help my client prepare for that important meeting. Or, as a third example, it might happen when a client is hit with a crisis — say, the loss of his job — and could use some support. At such times, I am happy to engage in a little email coaching between sessions, at no charge.

To repeat, not all coaches would want to do this. It takes time; it takes effort; it is unpaid work; and it can prove unsettling and downright difficult to try to help in times of crisis and emergency. It is really rather generous to coach between sessions — and a lawyer, for one, would charge for every one of those minutes spent reading emails and crafting replies. I think the key is whether or not you find this easy to do. If it feels burdensome, there is no need for you to burden yourself in such a way. But if you find it easy and even enjoyable, well, your clients would certainly appreciate your added attention.

If you do decide to coach between sessions via email, the key is not to say too much when you reply. You would pick one or two useful things to say and keep your reply to that. This makes less work for you than if you were to write a tome, and it is also easier for a client to digest and use. Your client may write a lot, but that doesn't mean that you have to reply in kind. Rather, make your reply strategic, compassionate, helpful, and short.

If you find that you are exchanging emails too often with a given client, you would find your way of saying, "Let's continue this the next time we chat." It takes a bit of courage and skill to press "pause" on the coaching in this manner, but it is a skill you can learn, and, hopefully, it is courage you can muster. Just be friendly, careful, and direct.

Personally, I enjoy coaching a little between sessions, and I know that it benefits clients. But I'm also aware that to coach between sessions, without being paid for my time and energy, might strike you as something you do not want to do or even as something you don't see as appropriate to do. Plus it is much safer not to coach between sessions — there's no chance of you saying the wrong thing if you are saying nothing! On the other hand, though, you might just enjoy it...

As with the other ideas I'm presenting, I'd ask you to just give it a little thought. A little coaching between sessions is absolutely not a "should." But maybe it falls in the category of the occasional lovely good deed? It is certainly something worth pondering.

Easy. Consider the question "Do I think that I would like to coach between sessions via email?"

Easy. Say, "I can decide to coach or not to coach between sessions."

Medium. List the pros and cons of coaching between sessions. Where do you land?

High bar. Picture a hypothetical client with whom you've been working for some time. Imagine her dropping you an email between sessions, asking for your advice. How do you feel reading that email? How do you think you would react and respond?

Food for Thought for Informal Coaches

You are informally coaching someone with whom you meet regularly. Something comes up in his or her life between your regularly scheduled meetings. How might you like to handle emergencies of this sort?

Writing Prompt for Self-Coaches

Write to the prompt "Things will naturally come up in life. Lots of things. I can picture coaching myself in such situations in the following way..."

26

Starting Fresh or Continuing?

You've met with your client once. Maybe you've been in contact with her between that first session and your upcoming second session, because you invited her to check in with you periodically and she has or because you've been doing a bit of email coaching between sessions. Now, you have a second session scheduled. How should you conceptualize this second session?

Are the two of you starting fresh, because it makes sense to articulate the basic issues a second time? Or are the two of you continuing, building upon and learning from that first session, from any interactions you've had between sessions, and from the work your client has done or attempted to do between sessions? Or maybe you're doing both, starting fresh *and* continuing? I think that the answer is both.

To turn this "both" into two monologues, which a coach would likely never actually deliver, might sound like this.

Monologue 1

"The last time we met, we got three or four goals articulated. Let me repeat them, to make sure I've got them right. You wanted to work on creating a healthier lifestyle. You wanted to do something to help yourself sleep better. You wanted to get out of your current job and find a job that better suits your needs. And you wanted to reconnect with that novel you started writing a couple of years ago. Is that about right?"

Monologue 2

"Okay, with regard to that last goal, we agreed that you'd try to get to your desk five days a week, first thing each morning, and write for thirty minutes. But when you checked in, it was clear that that plan wasn't working so well, so we tried the simple change of reducing those thirty minutes to twenty minutes. Did that help? Did that make any difference?"

A second session is part summarizing a client's initial presentation of their challenges and desires; part looking carefully at how the interval between session one and session two went (which interval may have been a week, two weeks, or a month); part examining your client's challenges in light of how that interval went; and part plotting new strategies that take into account what was learned during the interval and what insights percolate up in session.

This isn't a linear affair, but it does have some natural and logical linear energy to it. To put it in a sentence, it sounds like: "Let's first remind ourselves about what brought you to coaching, let's see how this first month went, and let's see what we've learned from this first month that can help us as we move forward."

Very often step two, checking in on the month, will come before step one, summarizing. This might sound like:

You: "Good to see you!"
Client: "Good to see you, too."
You: "Catch me up a little. How has the month gone?"

And your client will start where he or she wants to start. Then, at some natural and appropriate point, you might say, "Okay, I think we have a good sense of how the month went with regard to the songwriting. Can we touch base on the other goals you set? I believe they were the following three..." And you would summarize.

We'll look at the second session in more depth in a moment. But this is a good starting point. The second session is like the first session in that a client's challenges and goals get named again. It is different from the first session in that time has passed between two sessions, during which time your client did, or intended to do, certain things. If we hold space for both, we will have a rich second session.

EXERCISES

Easy. Sit with the phrase "second session." What comes up for you?

Easy. What might be a minimum outcome from a second session, something not necessarily grand but nevertheless valuable?

Medium. Visualize a second session. What are you seeing? What are you feeling?

High bar. Can you describe in your own words how a second session might differ from, but also be similar to, a first session?

Food for Thought for Informal Coaches

Picture meeting with someone you're informally coaching. How might you go about summarizing "where the two of us are at"?

Writing Prompt for Self-Coaches

Picture your ongoing self-coaching work around some issue. Write to the prompt "Each time I return to self-coaching around that issue, I might begin by summarizing in the following way..."

27

Checking In on the Interval

Let's say that you've set up your coaching as a once-a-week sort of thing or a once-a-month sort of thing. Maybe you've chosen once a week because you want the income that more frequent sessions would provide, or maybe you've chosen once a month because you want to pay attention to your other life purposes, in addition to coaching clients. In any event, you've set up your interval and aren't looking to change it.

Even though you aren't looking to change it, you still need to make sense of it with regard to each individual client. If you are meeting weekly with clients, some clients will feel that sessions are happening too often. If you are meeting monthly with clients, some clients will feel that sessions are happening too infrequently. And with each client, you will need to appraise how well the particular interval you've chosen is working and what changes you might want to make, not to the interval but to your coaching expectations.

Say that you are meeting weekly with a client who isn't meeting her goals. You sense that it is disturbing her, and not really serving her, to have to report every single week that she has yet again not met her goals. What to do? Well, you might say something like, "You know, the weeks are zipping by awfully quickly. I wonder, maybe we should set a two-week goal rather than a one-week goal? Maybe that's a better idea? Of course, we'll check in on it next week. But maybe that doesn't have to be our main focus next week?"

Or say you are meeting monthly with a client who is reporting some progress but who seems a bit absent and distant, a bit hard to pin down, and a bit reticent in session. You may have the suspicion that something is going on in your client's life that he isn't sharing with you, and you may have the fear that if you wait another whole month before chatting again, you will grow even further apart. What to do? Well, you might say something like, "You know, I'm experiencing a month as a very long time between chats. I wonder, maybe you'd like to begin to check in with me weekly, so that we stay connected? How does that sound?"

It is good to engage in this sort of appraising even as soon as the second session. What's your first impression? Did your client seem to experience that first week as a nice amount of time in which he got a lot done? Or did it seem to pass in a blur, at the speed of light? If the former, you might confidently cocreate equally ambitious goals for the coming week. If the latter, you might suggest a bit of a scaling back or even a significant scaling back. Your appraisal naturally affects what you focus on in that second session, as you are either slowing him down, keeping him at the same pace, or speeding him up.

EXERCISES

Easy. Ponder the following odd question: "Do I experience a month as four times as long as a week?"

Easy. Say, "For any given client, I will be able to intuitively gauge how the interval is working."

Medium. Call a big project to mind. What feels like a one-week goal with respect to that project, and what feels like a one-month goal?

High bar. Set yourself an ambitious goal with a one-week deadline. Picture in your mind's eye the way your week is likely to pass. Can you see yourself tackling the work you set for yourself, tackling only a portion of it, or maybe not getting to it at all? Does it feel like the goal was correctly framed as a one-week goal, or would it have been better to tweak it in some way? If you have the patience and the energy, run the same mind experiment on a one-month goal and see how that plays itself out.

Food for Thought for Informal Coaches

Picture someone you are informally coaching. Ask yourself the question "Am I maybe meeting with this person too frequently? Or maybe too infrequently?" See what comes up for you.

Writing Prompt for Self-Coaches

Write to the prompt "I wonder, do I prefer to set myself one-week goals or one-month goals? If I prefer one to the other, what's that preference about?"

28

Beginning to Calibrate the Pace

You will already have gotten a sense in your first session as to whether you're going to be moving relatively quickly or relatively slowly with a given client. But the second session gives you another, and better, opportunity to calibrate the pace of your work together. Your client has now had a week, two weeks, or a month to work on her goals. Her report on her experience of that time will go a long way toward how you decide at what pace to proceed.

Let's say she reports that she's written every day on her screenplay and feels energized and enthused. That's a rather amazing outcome and cause for a round of applause. It also likely signals that you and your client can move rather quickly together. But if, by contrast, she reports that she's managed to write only two or three days during the month and hated her output on those days, you would likely relax into the understanding that you may need to go slowly here — even very slowly.

In session, the main difference between the two is that in the second scenario you will be focusing on the past — on the month that was — and in the first scenario you will get to look to the future, to the contours of the coming month.

Moving slowly might sound like this:

You: "Ah, that's too bad. What seemed to be getting in the way?"
Client: "I think it's that I have no idea what the screenplay wants to be about."

You: "What had you thought it wanted to be about?"

Client: "I thought it was going to be about my grandmother, about her hard life in Ireland, her heroism, her...martyrdom."

You: "And?"

Client: "And it seemed to want to be more about me."

And so you would proceed, calmly, patiently, and slowly, sitting with your client as she makes sense of her shifting screenplay.

On the other hand, moving quickly might sound like this:

You: "So you got a lot done. That's great! Tell me about it."

Client: "I wrote just about every day! And I'm pretty sure I know what's going on with the script."

You: "Great! Okay, let's look ahead. Given how this month has gone, when might you have a draft done?"

Client: "Wow! Do we get to think about that already?"

You: "No reason not to. You're moving right along, so let's get a picture of what a nice high bar goal might look like. If you continued at this pace, when might a draft be done?"

Client: "Well...three months feels about right."

You: "Okay!"

Remember that there is no absolute principle involved here, that you should always go slowly or that you should always pick up the pace. Whatever sort of coaching you're providing — life coaching, spiritual coaching, executive coaching, health coaching, et cetera — you will feel this sort of difference in session, that with one client you must go slowly and that with another client you can pick up the pace. You decide on the pace contextually.

The pace will be different from client to client. But it will also routinely vary with the same client. You may have to go slowly with a client because she doesn't know what the screenplay that she is attempting to write is about; but once she does know, she may bring a lot of pent-up energy and enthusiasm to the writing enterprise, and you might find the pace naturally quickening. Conversely, a client may be making real and rapid progress, and then something unfortunate happens and the pace must slow dramatically to meet her changed prospects, circumstances, or mood. Pace is not a constant sort of thing, even with a single client or within a single session.

Easy. Say, "*Pace* suggests running a race. But there is no race."

Easy. Picture yourself effortlessly slowing down in session and effortlessly speeding up in session. Picture what that looks like and how that feels.

Medium. Do you have a sense of what your natural preference is, to go slow or to go fast? If one is your natural preference, how will you cultivate the other one?

High bar. Picture a hypothetical client session, one where you realize that you had better go slowly. How would you slow the pace? Then, picture a second hypothetical client session, one where you realize that you can pick up the pace. How would you do that?

Food for Thought for Informal Coaches

Are you pretty good at telling when you can move quickly with someone you're informally coaching and when you need to move more slowly? What might help you get better at discerning which is needed?

Writing Prompt for Self-Coaches

Write to the prompt "When I can move more quickly, I will. When I need to move more slowly, I will. I will keep this idea in mind by…"

29

Expanding and Amplifying

You have now learned a lot about your new client and his needs, from the information you received before the first session, from your interactions with him in the first session, and perhaps from check-ins between the first and second sessions. The second session begins; and you start to learn even more.

Now you learn that he didn't work on one of his goals, building his jewelry business, because he's waiting on a home remodel to be completed, which will take another three months (he hopes) and which will include a new space for his jewelry business; because both a favorite aunt and his pet golden retriever recently passed away and he is still mourning their deaths; and because his husband, whom he hasn't brought up before, has again been belittling his efforts at selling his jewelry. Hearing all this may make you feel less sanguine about your client's chances; but you do have additional crucial information to go on.

You have an expanded picture of your client's situation, and you would now need to do one of those two things that a coach is always doing: you would either invite your client to pick a direction for the conversation to go, based on these considerations; or you would pick a direction, because you have a hunch about which would be the most productive direction to pursue or the most important issue to investigate.

The former might sound like: "Okay! It's good to know all that.

Where do you think we should focus: on the remodel, on your recent losses, or on your husband? What are your thoughts?" The latter might sound like: "Ah, you know, in my experience folks who wait on a remodel to get finished before they get on with their work often find themselves waiting a *very* long time. Remodels have a way of going on and on. I wonder, is there any way the jewelry business can move forward while the remodel is still going on?"

You will respond in one of these two ways — and you will learn even more. The picture of your client's concerns and circumstances will keep expanding. In one session, you'll learn that his adult son committed suicide. You'll take that in. In another session, you'll learn that he spent three years in India in an ashram. You'll take that in. In another session, you'll learn that his small jewelry pieces sell very well but his larger pieces hardly sell at all. You'll take that in. It isn't that every time you learn something, you'll stop to comment or pause to recalibrate the coaching. But something will register, and something will shift.

Not every bit of information is a bombshell. You aren't continually changing your mind about where to go or what to do. Rather, you are seeing ever more clearly; and that clarity will naturally influence — and deepen — the work. Imagine, for instance, that your client lets drop that he has seven grandchildren, none of whom live nearby. Wouldn't that plant a seed and sprout when next you chatted about why he is so down about not being able to travel? These expansions and amplifications are the life blood of coaching.

EXERCISES

Easy. Say, "I can deal with receiving more and more information about my client and his situation."

Easy. Say, "That the coaching expands and amplifies is perfectly natural and perfectly okay."

Medium. If you make notes about clients and add new information during or after sessions, what will you do with those notes? Realistically, when and how frequently might you revisit them? Or will you keep client notes in your head? How might that work?

High bar. Picture that you and your client are together for a second session, she says something important, and in the moment, you aren't sure whether to stop and investigate or to go with the flow already established. Feel through two possibilities: that you stop the session and that you don't stop the session. What are your thoughts about how each of these makes you feel?

Food for Thought for Informal Coaches

Picture an informal coaching situation. The person you're coaching suddenly provides you with some quite new information. What will you do with it?

Writing Prompt for Self-Coaches

Write to the prompt "Whenever I gain some new insight into what's going on, I'm going to turn that insight into action steps by..."

30

Narrowing and Focusing

It is not at all unusual for me to spend a whole session with a client on one seemingly small thing. Say that I'm coaching a writer who's working on a fantasy novel and can't decide which of her two main characters *is* the main character. The princess seems like the logical choice, for obvious reasons, but the princess's personal bodyguard, a mysterious warrior woman, seems the rather more interesting character. Who shall it be?

My client and I might well spend a great deal of this session hashing this out, for the simple, poignant reason that she can't really make much progress on her novel until she knows who her main character is. To reach her goal, this must get addressed; and if we can solve this problem in session, that would be a session well spent.

Often, in session, we shine a bright light, aim our microscope, narrow our gaze, and focus on something very particular:

- Maybe you're a health coach, working with a client on their eating habits. You might focus a significant chunk of a session just on discussing healthy snacks.
- If you're a business coach or an executive coach, you might spend a good bit of time on a single important conversation that your client will have with his boss in the upcoming week.
- If you're a life coach working with a client complaining of

chronic fatigue, you might spend a whole session on her bedtime routine, angling toward helping her get a better night's sleep.

• If you're a spiritual coach or existential coach working with a client who is trying to make sense of his meaning needs, you might spend real time examining a certain past experience to try to understand why your client found it meaningful.

To focus on snacks, a single conversation, your client's bedtime routine, or one past experience is not to focus too narrowly. It may be exactly what you and your client need to be talking about and exactly where you need to be together. And if that conversation takes up virtually the whole session, so be it. As long as you've begun the session by checking in and monitoring your client's progress, and as long as you end the session summarizing and making sure that your client knows what she or he is intending to do next, it is perfectly fine to spend the bulk of the session on something as small as snacks or bedtime routines.

To summarize a bit: during this second session, you are both starting fresh and continuing; checking in to see how much got done or didn't get done in the past week, two weeks, or month; beginning to calibrate your working pace; and expanding and amplifying and/or narrowing and focusing the coaching. This may sound like a lot, but it is all rather easy, once you get the hang of it.

These are natural parts of an organic process, as natural as trying to help a friend understand her next steps after a divorce (where, to take one example, you might decide to remind her how important it's going to be to budget) or trying to help your teenager think about college options. In these situations, we know that we are not expecting perfect solutions or complete resolution; we simply hope to be of some real help. That is what coaching is about, and that is what your second session with your client is about.

Easy. Say, "Focusing in session on something seemingly small is perfectly permissible."

Easy. Say, "Nothing is too small to focus on, if it's useful or important."

Medium. Picture a session with a hypothetical client. You have been spending a good bit of time on a small matter. How is that feeling?

High bar. Do you suspect that you will have some internal objections to focusing on seemingly small matters, maybe because you harbor the belief that you should be doing more or maybe because you get easily bored and worry that chatting about small issues will bore you? If you do harbor internal objections, try to address them.

Food for Thought for Informal Coaches

Do you harbor a prejudice against detail work? Can you have a conversation with yourself about that?

Writing Prompt for Self-Coaches

You don't want to get lost in the weeds. At the same time, you want to pay attention to whatever is important, even if it feels very small. Write to the prompt "I can walk the line between getting lost in the weeds and paying attention to what matters by…"

31

Quality Quiet

Quiet has different feels to it, depending on the circumstances. If you're in a car accident and you dial 911, when the 911 operator asks you, "What's your location?" you will likely fall silent as you gather your wits and try to figure out where you are. That pulsating silence has a very different quality to it than the silence you experience when you read a book in a quiet room.

Quality quiet is a rare commodity nowadays. Noise is everywhere, and only a fraction of it is audible. A busy video game, with all its pulsations and animations, is noisy even if and when you mute it. There is all that noise of emails, social media, flashing advertisements, blog posts, and the never-ending whirl of bytes and electrons. There is even the noise of nature — the pounding of waves, the croaking of toads, the clicking of crickets — which for some does not make the experience of being outside a quiet or a peaceful one. If even nature is noisy, where is there quiet?

In session. In session, we aim to produce a certain sort of quiet that reads as "Everything is okay. We can take the time to look at this. There's no rush. Feeling takes time. Thinking takes time. Let's be quiet together and work on whatever we need to work on in some good, generous, quality silence."

Say that you make the following observation while working with an actor.

You: "It doesn't seem like you've been highly motivated to audition?"
Client: "No, I haven't."
You: "What do you think might create some motivation?"

This is one of those questions that we then follow with deep, quality quiet. Clients can sense if we are pulling for some quick fix answer — really, a way for both of us to get out of this awkward moment — or are instead holding a space for some real and even painful reflection. Clients understand the difference and really appreciate quality quiet.

It isn't that a client or a coach must stay still or silent for a certain number of seconds. It isn't the amount of quiet that follows such a question that matters, but rather the quality of that quiet. What can such a phrase as "the quality of quiet" possibly mean? Yet we understand very clearly differences among (1) no room for quiet, (2) token, breathless quiet (with its demand that someone say something soon), and (3) deep quiet (with its real permission to go on for as long as it needs to last). Let us add the phrase "quality quiet" to our vocabulary and have this be one of those things that we come to understand deepens every encounter with clients.

EXERCISES

Easy. Be with the thought "I can be quiet."

Easy. Where do you experience real, deep, quality quiet?

Medium. What do you think would help produce the experience of quality quiet in session, and what might get in the way of that quality quiet happening?

High bar. Visualize a coaching situation where something comes up that might normally pull you to respond immediately. Visualize not responding and instead remaining peaceful and quiet. How does that feel? Nerve-racking? Doable? Nerve-racking *and* doable? Or…?

Food for Thought for Informal Coaches

Do you informally coach in a noisy environment? Is there anything that can be done about that?

Writing Prompt for Self-Coaches

Write to the prompt "I can create quality quiet in my own life and in my own mind by…"

32

Shared Silence

There is a world of difference between shared silence and forced silence. Folks sometimes fall silent because they are forced to. They also fall silent for all sorts of personal reasons: because, for instance, they are lost in thought or because they are taking in a hushed landscape. They also sometimes fall silent because they are solemnly sharing silence with another person. These three silences — forced silence, personal silence, and shared silence — feel dramatically different one from the other.

To begin with, where do we encounter forced silence? Well, to take one example, I regularly teach at a workshop center where, if you eat in the main hall, you must be silent at breakfast. (You can take your breakfast elsewhere, if you want to chat.) Folks take this injunction very seriously. The main hall at breakfast is full of silence, to be sure, but to my ear it is a pressure-filled silence, not a peaceful quiet. I prefer not to be there.

There are many places where silence is forced upon you: in court, during a sermon, at the conference center I just mentioned, and so on. You may have experienced it at your family dinner table ("Your father needs peace and quiet!"), in the car on family trips, or when visiting relatives. Even the silence at the symphony or the opera is a variety of forced silence, where a cough gets you a dirty look or an actual scolding. We have all experienced being forced to keep quiet.

We also know what it's like to fall silent for personal reasons.

Maybe there's a political conversation going on around us, and we know that we do not want to get involved. We fall silent and stay silent. Maybe there's a gathering of gossips at the watercooler, and we don't want to participate in that chat. We fall silent and stay silent. We also might fall silent because we want to avoid disputes, because we're lost in thought, and for all sorts of other reasons.

Then there is shared silence, the sort of silence we witness when we watch a long-married couple strolling along during their afternoon walk. They have permission to speak but no need to speak. Maybe they still hold hands; maybe they are thinking the same thing; maybe they are thinking different things. And occasionally one might say to the other, "What are you thinking?" But for the most part, they are simply sharing the day, sharing the walk, and sharing the silence.

And where do we regularly experience this third sort of silence? In session.

Shared silence in session is something to cultivate. You want your client to feel comfortable being quiet for a moment, and *you* want to feel comfortable falling silent for a moment. You don't want silence to frighten you or to cause you to press ahead just for the sake of filling the airwaves. If, for example, your client is flooded with feelings as a result of something that has come up, you want to be able to be with her quietly without feeling the need to say something. This shared silence is an important thing, a beautiful thing, and it deepens your relationship with your client.

Sessions are full of words, thoughts, and energy. But they should also have their moments of shared silence. These are yours to cultivate.

EXERCISES

Easy. Say the phrase "shared silence." Just be with the phrase and with any feelings that come up as you say it.

Easy. Say, "I can be easy with shared silence."

Medium. When and where have you experienced shared silence with another person? What was your experience like? If you experienced it as powerfully positive, why do you think that might have been the case?

High bar. Get a hypothetical client in mind. The two of you are chatting, and something comes up that requires that both of you stop and think for a moment. How might you frame your invitation to share some silence?

Food for Thought for Informal Coaches

How might you interpret what shared silence means in the context of your informal coaching?

Writing Prompt for Self-Coaches

Write to the prompt "In order to create some occasional shared silence, I would need to…"

33

Shifting into Empty

Rather often in a session, you may find yourself pressing. Maybe it's one of those moments when you're offering suggestions and each one seems to be falling flat or, worse, seems to be offending your client. Or maybe it's a different sort of moment, when you're wanting to drop in an exercise, teach something, or make a point, but you can't find the right moment and feel caught between the need to listen and the impulse to interrupt. Or maybe you're tired of hearing this particular story one more time, and either you want to say something, anything, so as to change the channel or else you find your mind wandering very far away. These moments can and do happen.

What to do? A good policy is to shift into empty. You've gotten hooked in some way — hooked offering suggestions, hooked wanting to teach something, hooked into a feeling of boredom or restlessness — and you can unhook easily if you learn to clear your head, let everything go, and come back to the present moment. You hush your own mind; release your desires, your worries, and even your intentions; and blissfully feel all the mental chatter evaporate.

You may also have to say something — maybe something like, "I've been offering a lot of suggestions. But I'm not sure that offering suggestions is exactly what's needed at the moment. Let me take a break from that, and let's see where we want to go next." Then you allow for some quality quiet. Maybe you even shut your eyes for a moment. You signal to your client that this gentle interlude is available to the two of you, that you can go to this quiet place when and as needed. This welcome signal will help both of you calm down, regroup, and find the next place to be.

This emptying is its own form of leadership. You are modeling to your client the notion that not every second of the session has to be about doing, rushing, or pushing. You are leading the way a silent monk might lead a procession of monks or the way a parent might stop talking when she senses that it is time to just hug her child. It is quiet, but it is leadership.

Some helpers can stay in empty like this for a very long time and even have that as their main way of being in session. Nondirective Rogerian therapy (based on the work of the humanistic psychologist Carl Rogers) has that quality to it, where the therapist serves as a kind of voiceless echo chamber. The Rogerian therapist has a lot not to say. Similarly, many traditional Freudian and Jungian analysts stayed superhumanly quiet, only dropping in the occasional interpretation. A cavalry officer may lead by yelling, "Charge!" A coach, by contrast, may lead by shifting into empty and becoming very quiet.

What the coach is saying to himself at such moments is, "It is not helping my client that my head is full of noise. Therefore, I am making the conscious decision to quiet my mind, even though quiet can feel awkward. I am risking that awkwardness and accepting that awkwardness because I know that if I stay noisy inside, I won't be providing quality help. Okay, let me breathe, sigh, empty myself, and grow quiet — and present." You may not be able to do this yet, but it is a skill that is eminently learnable.

EXERCISES

Easy. Say the word *empty*. Say it and feel it.

Easy. Say, "I can shift into empty as needed."

Medium. Try putting into your own words what "shifting into empty" suggests or means to you.

High bar. In essence, I am asking you to do something that new meditation students find very hard to do. It is easy to say, "Empty yourself," but not necessarily easy to do. Let me invite you to practice this emptying and hold as a vision a time when this emptying will prove readily available to you, in session and in life.

Food for Thought for Informal Coaches

Informal coaching, like all coaching, comes with certain pressures — to perform, to make sense of the situation, not to upset the other person, to problem solve, to be of some real help, and so on. When you feel pressured in one of those ways, what might you do to release that pressure?

Writing Prompt for Self-Coaches

Write to the prompt "When I'm self-coaching and find I am pressing myself, I will..."

34

Quiet Thinking and Accelerated Thinking

As coaches, we engage in two kinds of thinking in session: what I'm calling "quiet thinking" and "accelerated thinking." These roughly correspond to being quiet in session, listening to your client, and safely holding the space so that he can say what's on his mind; and, alternately, speaking in session by asking a question, making an observation, making a suggestion, et cetera. Both of these modes should rightly be thought of as thinking since, when we are listening, we aren't tuned out or thinking our own thoughts. In both instances, we are using our brain in the service of our client's needs.

Let's take an analogy. Imagine that you are a medical doctor and your patient is telling you about his current medical issue. If you have the patience to quietly listen and not rush your patient along, then you will be doing two things simultaneously: you will be quietly listening and quietly thinking as he speaks, deciding in your own mind, and in your practiced experience, what does and does not pertain to the medical issue; and then, when he says something that sounds like a big clue that needs immediate investigating, you would move to a more active or accelerated thinking, with your brain suddenly engaging more of its skills, tools, repertoire of stored information, and energy. You had been quietly thinking all along; now, you are thinking in an accelerated way.

As a second analogy, say that you are an air traffic controller. You have many blips on the screen in front of you, all representing aircraft of one size or another, and you are definitely monitoring them, for the safety of all involved. You are engaged in a quiet, steady-state sort of thinking that could almost be called "not thinking." However, when you see one of those blips do something that, in your practiced experience, looks unusual and signals danger, you switch instantly to another mode of thinking that is more active, alert, and accelerated. You have been thinking all along, but now many more of your neurons are firing.

Quiet, energetic coaching has this same quality to it: you are quietly monitoring what your client is saying until you hear something that signals to you that you ought to ask a question, ask for clarification, make a suggestion, drop in an exercise, or in some other way move from quiet thinking to accelerated thinking. In neither case are you thinking your own thoughts, any more than the doctor is mentally writing a journal article as his patient speaks or the air traffic controller is paying her bills. Your own thoughts do not have a place here — if they do, you aren't really being present. Both your quiet thinking and your accelerated thinking are in the service of your client's needs.

Thinking is one of the universe's amazing things, and its amazingness can't be captured in phrases like "quiet thinking" or "accelerated thinking." These are very rough approximations of something extraordinary a brain can do, like getting us from one part of town to another part without our noticing that we are driving, or like solving a problem two weeks after we set ourselves the problem without our having consciously thought about it in between. This is the amazing brain that we bring to coaching, one that can think quietly as it listens and that can rouse itself to another level of thinking when it hears something to which it feels it ought to respond.

To employ a final metaphor, when you are driving along at the speed limit, you feel no sense of speed. But the engine is surely working, or you wouldn't be moving. Then, when you need to pass the slow-moving car in front of you, you must accelerate, and suddenly you experience the power of your engine. In both instances, the engine was working — but in the second instance, it moved to a new gear. We use our brain exactly this way in session: humming along quietly when no acceleration is needed and putting our foot to the pedal when that is what is required of us.

Easy. Say, "I can accelerate my thinking as needed."

Easy. Say, "Neither quiet thinking nor accelerated thinking makes me anxious."

Medium. Imagine conducting a session at only one speed, without any acceleration. How would that feel? Conversely, imagine conducting a session that was all acceleration. How would that feel?

High bar. Watch a video lecture on a subject that interests you. Notice how you are quietly listening and thinking until something is presented in the lecture that suddenly pulls you to accelerate your thinking. Can you describe what just happened? And what does that suggest for your coaching?

Food for Thought for Informal Coaches

How do you experience moving your thinking to another gear? Do you enjoy that? Does that stress you out? Do you experience some mix of agitation, anxiety, and enthusiasm? See if you can think through your relationship to both quiet thinking and accelerated thinking.

Writing Prompt for Self-Coaches

Write to the prompt "In order to learn more about my own ways of thinking, I think I will..."

35

Leading and Following

Consider a rather typical business meeting. The CEO asks everyone for their input. To all the world, it looks like an idea-gathering and fact-gathering meeting. Then, at the last moment, the CEO makes a pronouncement, the one that he had intended to make all along. Everyone in the room sinks under the weight of his proclamation, understanding that the meeting was for show. It looked, until the last minute, like a lovely idea-gathering adventure; and it turned out to be a waste of time.

Coaching isn't anything like that. Coaches see their work as a collaborative dance of genuine following, where what the client has to say really matters, and careful, thoughtful leading, where the coach's knowledge, expertise, and wisdom have their part to play. The phrase "quiet, energetic presence" captures something of the character of this elegant dance. A coach fosters quality quiet as she listens, nods, and thinks; and, when it is called for, she accelerates her thinking, ups her energy, and does her active part.

Say that your client is explaining that "nothing is getting done." The laundry isn't getting done; building her home business isn't getting done; her tasks as executor of her father's estate aren't getting done; important home repairs aren't getting done; practicing the cello isn't getting done. You are quiet as you hear this. You are also quietly asking yourself the question, "What might help a little with all this?" You are inhabiting her world, looking around, and silently and sympathetically wondering, "Hmm, given all this, where might we go?"

At some point, it is your turn. Maybe your client has provided you with an opening by having come to the end of her litany, by repeating herself in a way that you know isn't helpful, or by coming to an abrupt stop, right in the middle of speaking, signaling that she can't go on. Now, you must pick up the ball. Your quiet thinking, the thinking you were doing as you followed her story, now must transform itself into energetic leadership.

It won't quite do to say, "Tell me more" or "How does that make you feel?" Nor will it do to apply a label from on high — for instance, "Yes, you have nothing-getting-done-itis. There's a treatment for that." It is on your shoulders to do a bit of leading by marshaling your thoughts and saying something like, "Does any one thing connect all of this?" or "Which of these should we look at more closely?" or "Has this been going on for a very long time?" or some other quality question that allows your client to catch her breath and that, hopefully, points the two of you in a useful direction.

In the next chapter, we'll look more closely at the idea of quality questions. Introducing those is one form that your leadership may take. You might also make what in therapy has traditionally been called an "interpretation" — you might hazard a guess at what's underneath the litany. This might sound like, "I wonder, might some heightened anxiety be operating here? Are you feeling more anxious these days than usual?" Your client will either say yes, no, or "I'm not sure" or else will offer up an alternative explanation, which might sound like, "No, I think it's despair, not anxiety." In this way, she will take the lead again, recalibrating the moment, and the two of you will dance on.

EXERCISES

Easy. Say, "I can lead, and I can follow."

Easy. When I say that leading and following are a sort of dance, what dance do you see?

Medium. Describe for yourself what "quiet energetic presence" might mean.

High bar. Try to think through if it feels easier for you to lead or easier for you to follow. What might you do to improve your willingness and/or your ability to lead or to follow, whichever is the more difficult for you?

Food for Thought for Informal Coaches

If you find yourself informally coaching, say at work, that likely means you are in a leadership position. Given that you are coming from that leadership position and given the folks you're informally coaching, how might leading and following work in your particular circumstances?

Writing Prompt for Self-Coaches

In life, do you prefer to follow the lead of others, or do you prefer to pick your own path and follow your own lead? Write to the prompt "Here are the places where I ought to follow more, and here are the places where I ought to lead more..."

36

What Is a Quality Question?

I want to help you come to a personal understanding of what it means to ask a quality question. A lot of coaching — a lot of life, for that matter — is about asking quality questions. What is a quality question? It is not the *only* right question to ask, as many sensible and useful questions can be asked in any given set of circumstances. Rather, it is a *top-tier* question that has the characteristic of being spot-on, that promotes engagement, and that pulls from our client the information or awareness that he or she really needs.

A doctor informs us that we have a serious illness. What's the spot-on, top-tier, quality question to ask? It's "What's the prognosis?" We aren't thrilled to be asking that question, and we dread her answer, but we know not to ask, "Where did you spend your summer vacation?" which would amount to a stall or a dodge. In this scenario, "What's the prognosis?" is the quality question to ask, and "Where did you spend your summer vacation?" is not. I'm sure you understand the difference.

A quality question goes wherever it is that you and your client need to go. It doesn't go elsewhere. It is almost always easier to go elsewhere, often reflexively, as in the therapist's classic "And how did that make you feel?" That "And how did that make you feel?" is sometimes a quality question, but more often than not it is a rote dodge, serving the therapist's need to say something. "And how did that make you feel?" and "What happened then?" and "Is that part of the same pattern?" are reasonable questions sometimes, but they are hardly ever as pointed, useful, or engaging as that hard-to-ask but important-to-ask question of the sort you put to your doctor: "What's the prognosis?"

Where does a quality question come from? It comes from you intuiting the major contours of the situation your client is presenting and asking a question that connects the dots. To be able to do that might sound preposterous on the face of it, and yet that can become surprisingly easy to do — easier, really, than plucking a more superficial question out of the air and asking it just for the sake of asking something.

That connecting of the dots is like you pulling together the facts that your child is abnormally silent, that he seems hungrier than he ought to be, given the big school lunch that you packed for him, and that he is having trouble looking you in the eye, then surprising yourself by asking, "Are you being bullied in school? Did someone take your lunch?"

Where did those two quality questions come from? From you noticing, thinking, discerning, and connecting the dots. To have asked, "How was your day?" or "Do you have a lot of homework?" would not have been spot-on. A quality question is not the only question that can be asked — there are likely many possible reasonable questions that can be asked in any given moment — but it is often *the* question to ask, the one unlike all the others, the one like "And what is the prognosis?" or "Are you being bullied?"

EXERCISES

Easy. How would you define a quality question?

Easy. Can you recall a quality question that you asked in some situation? What were the results?

Medium. Picture yourself in session. What might get in the way of you asking a quality question that you know you ought to be asking?

High bar. Get quiet, slip under the radar of your own defenses, and try to discern one or two quality questions to ask yourself. Then, ask them and answer them.

Food for Thought for Informal Coaches

Picture an upcoming informal coaching session. Do you have a quality question in mind that you might ask?

Writing Prompt for Self-Coaches

Write to the prompt "I will train myself to ask myself quality questions by…"

37

Three Possible Questions

Let me present you with a short scenario and follow it up with three possible questions a coach might ask. Let's see which of the three you think is the quality question.

A client of mine, a painter, is trying to decide whether to stay in Paris or move to the French countryside. There are reasons on either side of her decision, including that if she stays in Paris she will have to face her current creative project and if she flees to the countryside she can dodge her creative work for many months, and maybe for longer than that, as she gets settled.

She is pondering many considerations: that it will be much cheaper to live in the countryside; that she can have a bigger studio space in the countryside; that, on the other hand, she will likely feel more isolated in the countryside (and isolation is an issue); but she will have tremendous solitude; et cetera.

Many possible questions and roads of inquiry come to mind. Take the following three questions. All are solid. But which one feels like the quality question? And why?

- What are the pros and cons of this move?
- What might help you decide which is the better course of action?
- If you were to relocate, how would you attend to your creative work during the move?

To my mind, the third is the quality question. The first two questions are completely plausible and may help my client do some useful thinking and choosing. But to ask either of them is to collude a little in my client's wish not to be confronted about how her creative work will suffer if she makes this move.

To ask either of the first two is to act as if we haven't been working together, thinking together, and being together — they are questions a computerized coach might ask. The third question comes from a different place, from the place of a coach understanding (or believing that he understands) a deep reason for this move and then inquiring, in a gentle and compassionate but also straightforward and direct way, about the elephant in the room, my client's persistent avoidance of her creative life.

To repeat, there is nothing even slightly wrong with either of the first two questions. A client might well gain something for having been asked them. It isn't that the opposite of a quality question is a pointless question. The first two questions are useful and on point. But the third question, though provocative (as it is meant to be), builds on and incorporates the work that we've done and, in my estimation, does the most work in helping my client understand her own motivations.

It may also upset her. Quality questions often have that effect. That is a significant reason why we may shy away from asking them, just as we may shy away from asking our husband, "Is that your fifth glass of wine?" and shy away from asking our daughter, "Isn't that friend of yours always high?" A quality question typically challenges our client to deal with a real issue and bring into conscious awareness some painful reality. We therefore may not be thanked for asking it. But asking quality questions aligns with our twin goals of getting things on the table and trying to be of some help.

Because it may frighten you to ask quality questions, you may have to screw up your courage and practice asking them, maybe as part of some hypothetical scenarios that you create and play out in front of a mirror. I do hope that you'll encourage yourself to do this — it is that important.

Easy. Say, "I can ask the hard questions."

Easy. Say, "I can bravely ask any question that I deem important to ask."

Medium. What question would you personally prefer not to be asked? How would you feel if you were asked it? How might you react?

High bar. Create some hypothetical scenarios. Play them out in your imagination. Construct them so that a point arrives when you know that you ought to ask a quality question. See how it feels to ask it — and not to ask it. For those scenarios where you do ask your quality question, play out various client reactions, from guarded and defensive to open and thankful and anything in between.

Food for Thought for Informal Coaches

There is a serious difference between a quality question and criticism. Think of that old, on-point adage "The message received is the message sent." If you are consciously or subconsciously intending to be critical, that is how the person you are coaching will experience your question. If you aren't, she's much less likely to take your question as criticism. Try to get a good sense of what it feels like to deliver a quality question without a hint of criticism attached.

Writing Prompt for Self-Coaches

Write to the prompt "I would prefer not to be asked the following question..."

38

Handling Defensive Reactions

What may happen when we ask a quality question? Our client may get defensive. Remember the three questions from the last lesson, any one of which a coach might ask the painter-client I described? Here they are again:

- What are the pros and cons of this move?
- What might help you decide which is the better course of action?
- If you were to relocate, how would you attend to your creative work during the move?

The first two questions are not likely to provoke a defensive reaction. The third quite likely might. This might sound like the following.

Client: "I'm just not sure if moving to the countryside at this moment is or isn't a good idea."

You: "If you do relocate, how will you attend to your creative work during the move?"

Client (huffily): "Well, I'm sure I'll find a way! My painting is important to me! Just as soon as I get settled, I'll get right back to it!"

What now?

Even if we are thinking it, we certainly don't say, "No, you won't," or "I doubt it!" We meet defensiveness best by being agreeable and by resuming the work. This might sound like:

Client (huffily): "Well, I'm sure I'll find a way! My painting is important to me! Just as soon as I get settled, I'll get right back to it!"

You: "Great! But, of course, it would be good to have a plan in place for resuming the painting. What might that plan look like?"

Client: "Well..."

Even if your client is still bristling a bit, she is likely to follow your lead and begin to entertain the question of what a plan for painting in the midst of the moving tumult might look like. After a moment, she may say something like, "Well, I think the first thing would be to pick a painting spot, to dedicate some real space in the new place to the painting."

To which we would reply, "Great!"

We must allow clients to have their defensive reactions and not treat the situation as if we were being personally attacked or put under some sort of threat. Human beings get defensive — that is their right. It is our job as coaches to be helpful even at such times, which may mean not getting defensive ourselves and finding the way to cheerfully resume the work.

We needed to ask that quality, pointed, or difficult question, and we did. Now we must deal with our client's very natural self-protective reaction. Nothing terrible has happened — only something a little bit edgy. The moment will pass, and the work will continue.

EXERCISES

Easy. Say, "I can deal lightly and effortlessly with a client's natural defensiveness."

Easy. Picture yourself internally smiling, rather than tensing up or growing defensive yourself, in situations where your client's defensiveness has been activated.

Medium. When do you get defensive? How does that feel?

High bar. Create one or more hypothetical scenarios where you come to a choice point and might ask a quality question but worry about your client's reaction. Picture yourself bravely asking that question, even though you are nervous. Imagine being met with a defensive, bristling reply and working lightly and agreeably through and past that moment. Go through that whole cycle, reaching the point where a quiet footing has been restored and the work has resumed.

Food for Thought for Informal Coaches

It isn't wise to suppose that the folks we informally coach won't have natural human reactions. They may respond defensively; they may get upset; they may get angry; they may dig their heels in. What do you need to do to help yourself face such natural human reactions with some equanimity? Is there a pep talk that you need to have with yourself?

Writing Prompt for Self-Coaches

We human beings employ all sorts of defenses and give them names like "intellectualization," "rationalization," "denial," "projection," "displacement," et cetera. There are lots of ways that we defend ourselves! Write to the prompt "I think I would describe my personal defensive style as primarily..."

39

Practiced Not Understanding

It's important that coaches don't act as if they understand something that a client is wrestling with unless and until they do understand. Generic clarifying questions like "Can you tell me a little bit more about that?" and specific clarifying questions like "Can you tell me a bit more about not asking your boss for that raise we discussed?" are quality questions that often help our clients go deeper and help us better understand what they are facing.

In psychiatry, to take one example of a field where there is a rush to act as if you understand long before you really do understand, the practitioner is trained to come up with a "diagnosis" almost immediately and certainly by the end of the first session. How can he write a prescription if he hasn't quickly affixed a label? Rarely would a psychiatrist say, "I don't understand." With a checklist in hand, he finds understanding easy, as easy as ticking boxes off a list.

Coaches prefer not to act as if they understand until they do understand. They may well have some thoughts about what's going on, but those are hypotheses, intuitions, hunches, or guesses and not settled conclusions, not until they know enough. They invite their client to tell them more, so that the two of them can better understand. This helps a client gain insight into her situation and helps a coach know in what direction to take the coaching.

This is a particular sort of not understanding, one that is very different from the kind of not understanding that is just criticism. When someone says, "I just can't understand why you did that!" they don't mean, "Please tell me more so that I can understand." What they are implying is the relationship-destroying "I can't understand how you could have been that stupid!" or "I can't understand why you don't do what you say you'll do!" Utterances of this sort aren't genuine questions; they are accusations.

By contrast, a coach's "I don't understand" is the empathetic, compassionate, curious not understanding that sounds like, "I'm not quite understanding how that happened. Can you tell me more?" or "Wow, that's complicated! Can you unravel that a bit for me?" Your question is a real invitation, one that you might follow with some quality quiet time as you give your client a chance to think.

This is so valuable a way of inquiring that coaches may engage in a kind of practiced not understanding even when they think they do have a pretty clear picture of the situation. Say you have a good idea that when your client's husband criticizes her, that ruins her motivation to get her creative work done. Practiced not understanding here might sound like, "You found that you had the time this week to paint, but you didn't manage to get to the studio. Can you help me understand what happened?"

Maybe your client will identify her husband's criticism as the culprit, and maybe your supposition will be proven correct. But it still will have been good to double-check and to give your client the chance to go in the direction of her choosing. The better the job you do of not shutting the door on inquiry, the more both of you will understand. Sometimes you will not understand, and you will inquire; and sometimes you may believe that you do understand, and you will still inquire, so as to verify your belief and deepen your mutual understanding.

Easy. Say, "I feel at ease not understanding until I do understand."

Easy. Say, "Not knowing will no longer make me feel uncomfortable."

Medium. Is there something that you claim to understand but that you don't really understand? Sit with the discomfort of that truth.

High bar. Picture a hypothetical scenario where, despite all the information that your client has provided and all the talking that you two have done, you have the clear sense that you don't really understand what is going on. How might you proceed?

Food for Thought for Informal Coaches

Imagine that you are leading a team on a project and need to do some informal coaching with team members. Do you sense that you will come to these meetings with a "Let's get this solved!" energy or with a "Let me see if I understand?" energy?

Writing Prompt for Self-Coaches

Write to the prompt "Why do I claim to understand certain things when I know that I don't really understand them?"

40

The Art of the Experiment

Quality questions lead to useful experiments.

A quality question in physics is "What is time?" This question isn't an idle one — for example, GPS navigation will not work unless the fact that time slows down in the vicinity of large objects is taken into account. In science, when you pose a quality question like "What is time?" you follow that up with hypotheses about what time might be, hypotheses that then require testing. This is the experimental method.

Coaching works the same way. With a given client, a quality question might be "I wonder why you're able to paint on weekdays but not on the weekends?" This question might lead to several hypotheses: that your client's husband is home on the weekend, making demands; that during the week your client puts aside her chores and errands and saves them for the weekend; that her studio mates appear only on the weekend and their presence disturbs her; et cetera. These hypotheses would then naturally lead to experiments that you and your client would cocreate.

One experiment might be that she clearly announces to her husband that she intends to paint every Saturday morning and, having made that announcement, she sees if she then manages to get to the studio. A second experiment might be that she sets aside an hour every day to do chores, like the laundry, so that the chores don't pile up, and she sees if that makes a difference. A third experiment might be for her to go to the studio on the weekend, when her studio mates are there, tune them out by listening to music, and see if that does the trick.

The quality question led to hypotheses, the hypotheses led to the framing of experiments, and your client can now decide if she actually wants to run one or more of these experiments. It is up to her whether or not to run any at all and, if she does want to run one, which one to choose. But it is likely that she will pick one of them to run and also rather likely that she will actually run it. The experiments, framed as we framed them together, are not hard to understand and not complicated to run. And if one or another of them feels too risky to attempt — like, perhaps, making that announcement to her husband — she can always choose a safer-feeling alternative.

We have learned an amazing amount over the past several centuries by using the scientific method. Even in the "soft" social sciences, fascinating experiments have been run, producing eye-opening results. We have learned, for instance, the extent to which people are swayed by the opinions of those around them and the extent to which people will punish strangers just because they are told to do so. We have learned many hard truths about human nature via such experiments; and your client may also learn a hard truth or two by virtue of the experiments that she chooses to run. That may prove challenging, eye-opening, and positive all at once.

I find creating experiments and helping clients create experiments both easy and really enjoyable. You pose a quality question; hypotheses as to what may be going on arise from the ensuing conversation; and there you will find yourself, ready to brainstorm some experiments into existence. Relish that experience. You don't need advanced math, a billion dollars, or a particle accelerator to run coaching experiments: they are supereasy to create and supervaluable.

Easy. Say, "I am eager to cocreate experiments with my clients."

Easy. Put on the hat of an experimentalist. How does it feel?

Medium. Do you create experiments for yourself to run? Can you think of a recent one? How did it turn out?

High bar. Create a hypothetical scenario where a quality question has been asked and has led to the generation of a number of hypotheses. Try your hand at creating an easy-to-understand, easy-to-accomplish experiment to test each one of those hypotheses.

Food for Thought for Informal Coaches

Does your work involve the experimental method? If it does, how might you apply that method to your informal coaching?

Writing Prompt for Self-Coaches

Write to the prompt "I am going to go on the following interesting journey: I'm going to ask myself a quality question, dream up hypotheses based on that question, and then create experiments to run. And then I will run one of those experiments!"

41

The Art of the Drop-In

A medical doctor may have a certain exam routine that works for her and from which she rarely deviates. An estate lawyer may have his way of going over a will or a living trust with his clients. A baker may stick to their baguette recipe or their cinnamon bun recipe year after year. These routines make their logical sense, and no one would suggest to the doctor, lawyer, or baker that he or she do anything differently.

By contrast, take an inventor who is trying to solve a certain difficult problem in his head. One day he might sit at his laptop for hours on end. Another day he might swim laps. A third day he might watch old movies. A fourth day he might tinker with hands-on solutions, building models and, if they don't solve the problem, tossing them away. He may well have no set routine for inventing. Instead, he intuits what might work on a given day. His motto is "Process, not routine."

A coach is rather more like an inventor than like a doctor, lawyer, or baker. A session doesn't come with a road map, and you can't follow standard exam procedures or baguette recipes. You must improvise. Practically speaking, this may mean that right in the middle of the chat you are having with your client, you realize it might prove really helpful to stop everything and drop something in: maybe an exercise, an anecdote, a bit of teaching, a bit of rehearsing, et cetera. And so you do that.

You would do this for no other reason than that you think it makes sense to do so and you think it might help. Take the following scenario. Your client announces that she has finally gotten some literary agent interest in her memoir about her mountain-climbing experiences: an agent wants to chat with her next week about possible representation. Then she nervously rushes on to talk about an unrelated subject. This is a moment when a coach might well want to stop everything and say, "I wonder, do you have a good sense of what that agent might ask you? And how you would reply?"

Your client will almost certainly say, "No, I don't!" You might then decide to offer the drop-in of a dress rehearsal. I certainly would, because I know that my client would benefit from rehearsing. In fact, so important is that meeting with an agent, and so important is it to rehearse that meeting, that the ten or fifteen minutes we might spend rehearsing might make the entire difference between her garnering or not garnering representation.

Of course, you might not feel equipped to engage in this particular rehearsal. But imagine that you find yourself in an area that you know very well. Maybe, say, you are a trained mediator, and your client has an upcoming meeting that is analogous to a mediation. Might not that be useful to rehearse? Or say that your client is highly anxious about an upcoming audition, and you are trained in a certain anxiety-reduction technique. Might a little sharing and teaching not be in order?

In the following lessons, we'll look more closely at some possible drop-ins, like dropping in an exercise or stopping to do a bit of teaching. Here, let me repeat the headline. Baking rather demands that you follow the recipe. If you need yeast, you need yeast. But coaching rather demands that you think on your feet and respond spontaneously. You improvise in the interest of helping your client. Coaching is an inventive, creative enterprise — enjoy that about it!

Easy. Say, "I can improvise in session."

Easy. Think about a time you successfully improvised. Feel that success.

Medium. Feel through what it might be like to stop a session and make an invitation. Does that feel terrifying? If it does, what might help you relax into a willingness to improvise?

High bar. Picture a hypothetical coaching scenario. Get a good sense of what you and your client are working on. Now, create a moment where it might make sense to drop something in. See yourself doing that and working with your client in that way. If you can, relish the experience.

Food for Thought for Informal Coaches

When you informally coach, do you have a rule book you follow? Or are you obliged to improvise?

Writing Prompt for Self-Coaches

Write to the prompt "I think that I can use the idea of improvisation as it relates to my own self-coaching in the following way..."

42

Dropping in an Exercise

Most coaches have taken many trainings and many workshops in their lives; and even those who haven't are likely to have encountered exercises that they suspect might work well in session or might benefit their clients a lot.

However, they are typically reluctant to try out these exercises, for three reasons: they see them as a kind of forced intrusion, time waster, or shortcut in the session and not really legitimate; they haven't practiced their delivery well enough to offer their exercise suddenly and on the spot; and/or they don't know how to introduce the exercise in the middle of a real, live session.

I recently attended an online miniworkshop, presented by one of the coaches I was training, that lasted hardly more than ten minutes. The setup was simple: get in mind some problem you'd like to solve or some issue you'd like to address; listen to a piece of music (provided by the presenter); and see if anything about the problem or issue got clearer. Just that uncomplicated. And it worked!

Must you have some go-to exercises in your pocket because it's good to have backup and because you believe in them? No. Might you *want* to have some go-to exercises in your pocket because it's good to have backup and because you believe in them? Yes. This is not a "should," but it is a wise "might." The exercise might come from any world — the world of energy medicine, shamanism, cognitive therapy, mindfulness meditation — or from your own mind. And one coming from your own mind might well be the best.

Can the exercise you choose to use be someone else's exercise, something you encountered in a workshop or read about in a book? Of course. But it would be lovely if it were something you adapted, rather than used as is, or else something you created yourself. Such efforts at doing it yourself pay extra dividends and typically become resources you end up providing to the world in the form of books, classes, workshops, trainings, programs, a brand, and so on. So creating your own exercises has a tremendous upside.

You know what I'm going to ask you to do. I'm going to ask you to create an exercise...and to try it out. It is one thing to create an exercise, and that is a good thing. It is an even better thing to try your exercise out, bravely and even daringly, in session.

Picture how that might work. You and your client are discussing one of her goals, and she says something that reminds you that you have a short, on-point exercise at the ready. What to do?

You might say, "Ruth, let's stop for one moment. I have an excellent exercise that might help with what we're discussing. It takes about three minutes. Do you want to go there, or would you rather just continue?" Many times, your client will say, "I would really prefer to just continue." Then you smile, say, "Of course!" and continue. And sometimes your client will say, "I'd love that," and on you would go to the exercise.

Dropping in an exercise is exactly that simple. Yet it isn't really simple at all: you have to have an exercise at the ready, you have to bravely interrupt, and all the rest. But you can get very practiced at this — and then it *will* be simple.

EXERCISES

Easy. Think or say, "I can do brave, exciting things in session, like suddenly presenting an exercise."

Easy. Is an exercise a legitimate session drop-in? What are your thoughts, pro and con?

Medium. Think about your willingness or unwillingness to suggest an exercise to a client right in the middle of a session. What comes up for you when you consider that possibility?

High bar. Create an exercise suitable for dropping into a coaching session and actually drop it into a session.

Food for Thought for Informal Coaches

Do you employ exercises as part of your informal coaching? Might you like to include them?

Writing Prompt for Self-Coaches

Write to the prompt "I think I would like to create the following sort of exercise for myself..."

43

Stopping to Teach and Inform

Coaching is about many things: helping, leading, supporting, cheerleading, goal setting, and so on. It can also be about teaching. There is no prohibition against doing a little teaching in session, if the time is right and if the shoe fits.

What might you teach? In my world of creativity coaching, working with many writers who want to write or who are actively writing nonfiction books, I might stop and teach my client about the nonfiction book proposal, which is the sales tool of the nonfiction writer. I can teach the essentials of creating a strong book proposal, including a couple of top-level secrets, in ten minutes flat.

Not only is this a great boon to my client, who might otherwise have to take an expensive book proposal writing class and still not get what she needs, but also I enjoy it. I enjoy sharing what I know, and I enjoy the excitement it creates in my client, who, likely for the first time, suddenly has a clear sense of her next tasks as a nonfiction writer.

Do I have an agenda before a session that I am going to teach my client something? No. I have no teaching intentions as I enter a session. But if a moment arises when it makes sense to me to introduce something and to teach it, I will make that suggestion. This might sound like the following.

Me: "Well, it sounds like the next step in this project is to create a nonfiction book proposal. Do you know much about that?"

Client: "I've heard about it, but I have no real idea what that means."

Me: "Okay! Should we take a few minutes, and I can explain it to you?"

Client: "I'd love that!"

If my client says, "Let's do that another time," well, then that's that. I'll abide by her wishes, and we'll continue on the path that she wants to travel. But I likely will remind her near the end of the session, with enough time left to dive into it if she agrees, that she is going to need to create a nonfiction book proposal and that I do know a thing or two about that.

She may have been subconsciously processing my first mention of that task as we chatted about other things, and she may now be ready to hear more about it. In that case, I'll do a little teaching on the spot, before the session ends. And if she doesn't want to face hearing more about that task quite yet, so be it.

If, to take another example, my client and I are doing a little existential work, I might teach him what I believe to be the difference between making meaning and seeking meaning. If my client and I are chatting about health and weight loss, I might present a few ideas that I've found personally useful and that clients have found helpful — for instance, about menu planning, portion size, preparing snacks ahead of time, setting a time of the day after which no eating happens, et cetera. If we're chatting about how to move their career forward, I might make mention of the ideas of asking for what they want and asking for more. And so on.

Many of these ideas or suggestions don't amount to full-scale teaching. But they do require the coach, me, to feel free to introduce my own thoughts into the session. I do feel free to do that, because I know they can help. To begin with, you may find that hard to do, and you may rationalize your reluctance by internally announcing that "teaching has no place in coaching," as if somewhere a set of coaching laws were written in stone. But teaching does have its place. It is one of the hats that a coach can wear and sometimes an important one.

EXERCISES

Easy. Say, "I can teach and share information as needed."

Easy. Imagine that among the many coaching hats you wear is a teacher's hat. Put it on. How does it feel?

Medium. Do you have teaching experience, maybe as a teacher in a school or as a workshop leader at a retreat or conference center? If you do have that experience, has it been a good experience? Can you put yourself in mind of some pleasant teaching experiences?

High bar. Picture a hypothetical coaching session. Set it up so that a moment arrives when you could teach something that you know well. What might you say so as to stop the session and inquire of your client if she'd like to learn whatever it is that you have to teach? Mentally try out a few different ways of stopping the session and see which one feels the most congenial.

Food for Thought for Informal Coaches

It's quite likely that a part of your informal coaching involves teaching. If that's the case, are you prepared to teach what you need to teach? Or do you need to prepare yourself better?

Writing Prompt for Self-Coaches

Write to the prompt "I think that I need to teach myself..."

44

Back-Burner Matters

Say that I am working with a client on getting her novel written. Her life is chaotic, she rarely writes, she's in a battle with her brother over their father's small estate, a chronic illness is part of the picture, et cetera. All of that is on the front burner, so to speak. But there may also be pots on the back burners, ones that my client may not be monitoring but that I've decided to keep an eye on.

For instance, and as is often the case, this client may have a finished novel that she is no longer submitting to agents or editors, because it got rejected many times and consequently she feels defeated and doubtful of its chances. That finished-but-ignored novel is, from my client's point of view, completely off the stove. But I may have hopes for it, want to give it a chance at a life, and may well occasionally drop in mention of it.

This might sound like the following.

Client: "I'm thinking I may be working on the wrong novel. I think I'd love to take a break from it."

Me: "Okay. You mean, and not pester yourself about writing for a while? Or work on something different?"

Client: "I was thinking, maybe work on some short things?"

Me: "Okay. That makes sense. By the way, what about that novel set in an airplane? I think you said that with maybe one revision it could go out in the world again. Might this be a moment for tackling that?"

Most clients will say, "No!" in no uncertain terms. That is the last thing they want to do, revisit a project that still needs work and that proved such a disappointment. But every so often a client will say, "I could just possibly. I've actually been thinking about it a bit. Thanks for bringing it up!"

Even when a client says, "No!" clearly and adamantly, it still likely helps her in two ways that you brought the matter up. First, it reminds her that together the two of you can fearlessly look at the sore spots in her life. Second, and in a very practical way, it reminds her she has inventory available that, maybe with just a little tweaking or maybe without any tweaking at all, might just be wanted in the current marketplace. The publishing marketplace of ten years ago or even a year ago is nothing like the publishing marketplace of today, and her tabled novel may no longer need to be a sad reject but might, instead, suddenly be precisely of the moment.

To drop in a reminder about her tabled novel means that you've remembered its existence. As a coach, it can become part of your effortless practice to decide to remember a few back-burner matters in each of your client's lives: a tabled novel here, a long-simmering feud with a sister there, a desire to lose thirty pounds off in that corner. If you remember just a few of these matters with each client and bring them up occasionally, it can prove helpful, can give you a place to go if a session feels stalled, and can definitely deepen the coaching relationship.

EXERCISES

Easy. Say, "I can easily keep a few things in my back pocket with each client."

Easy. Say, "I have permission to bring up back-burner issues with clients."

Medium. Picture a session that has stalled a bit. Rather than feeling anxious or pressured to say something or do something, imagine feeling a certain ease and spaciousness as you remember something that you might bring up. Savor that ease and spaciousness.

High bar. Picture a stalled session. Somewhere in your memory banks, you have two or three stored memories of issues that you and your client haven't chatted about in a long time. Picture yourself remembering one of those issues and introducing it into the session. Can you see how that might work? Does that seem possible?

Food for Thought for Informal Coaches

If you do some informal coaching with a particular individual over time — maybe even a very long time — then it's likely things will come up that the two of you table and rarely return to. What would it be like if you took it upon your shoulders to return to one or another of these tabled matters, if you saw the chance and if it made sense to do so? Would that feel pushy? Or maybe quite helpful?

Writing Prompt for Self-Coaches

Write to the prompt "I know there are issues in my life that never quite get addressed, that always seem to get put on a back burner. I think I could do a better job of attending to these back-burner issues by..."

45

Monitoring Other Goals

You and your client may be working on something in particular as a primary goal. Maybe it's helping him advance up the ladder at work, change his relationship with his parents, or declutter his apartment. This is your main focus, and you rarely chat about anything else.

However, a time may come when you drop in a question about another one of your client's goals, one that perhaps got mentioned in his first email or in the first session but that hasn't surfaced again. This might sound like:

You: "You know, we were also maybe going to monitor your take on healthy eating. We haven't chatted about that in a while. How has that been going?"

Client: "That's completely on me. I haven't bothered at all to change my eating. I haven't had the motivation or the interest or the *anything* to deal with my eating."

You: "Should we take a look at that?"

Client: "I suppose."

Or it might sound like:

You: "You know, we were also maybe going to monitor your take on healthy eating. We haven't chatted about that in a while. How has that been going?"

Client (angrily): "Jack still has all the cupboards filled with his snacks! I can't get him to stop that no matter how much I nag."

You: "Okay. Let's tease that apart a bit. There's what you can't control: namely, Jack. There's what you can control: namely, you. What's in your control to do?"

Client (sourly): "Well, stop eating after six in the evening, like we discussed."

You: "Okay! Can we take a look at that?"

Client: "But there's still Jack!"

You: "Let's get back to Jack in a moment."

When you bring up something that your client at some point has deemed important and that you haven't chatted about for a long while, you can predict that she hasn't been attending to that something very much or at all. You can expect that, not have that surprise you, and not have that worry you. If you think it would be useful to air this subject, just go there, gently but directly. This may be exactly the right moment to revisit that something — in which case, you couldn't have spent a portion of the session more profitably.

You might come to a session ready to bring up one of your client's back-burner goals because you think it is time to revisit it. Or you might bring up that back-burner goal because the session is feeling a little stale, dry, or stalled. Or you might bring it up simply because it pops into your head to do so and because you have learned to trust your intuition on that score. Whether you bring it up because you intended to bring it up, because you feel the need to reenergize the session and the coaching, or because it has simply entered your mind, this solid option is available to you. Even if it has gotten relegated to a back burner, it *is* one of your client's stated goals — and deserves your mutual attention at least occasionally.

Easy. Say, "I can keep track of more than one client goal."

Easy. Say, "If a session stalls, I can bring up a back-burner goal."

Medium. Picture it popping into your head to revisit a client goal that the two of you haven't chatted about in a long time. Can you imagine stopping the session so as to introduce that topic? How does that feel?

High bar. Create a hypothetical client scenario where the two of you have been silently colluding in not looking at a stated client goal and where you know that bringing it up would prove edgy and provocative. Picture yourself preparing to bring it up, bringing it up, and dealing lightly and easily with the consequences of bringing it up. Picture a satisfactory, successful interaction.

Food for Thought for Informal Coaches

When you informally coach, do you tend to stay focused on a given topic, or is your coaching more far ranging than that? Is one way better than the other, or does it depend on the exact situation and circumstances?

Writing Prompt for Self-Coaches

Write to the prompt "I know that there's a subject I haven't chatted with myself about in some time, and I know why I haven't chatted about it. Let me chat with myself about it right now…"

46

The Art of Working Effortlessly

Things are easy only if they actually *do* feel easy. I remember traveling around Europe as a young man and getting a day laborer job hammering window frames in Ireland. Nothing could have felt harder, as I was deathly afraid of breaking the glass on those old, valuable windows. The folks around me hammered away happily and easily, and I got practically no work done. I lasted one day.

When would that have gotten easier for me? Maybe in a day or two...or maybe never. Sometimes things get easy with experience, and sometimes things never do get easy. Many great performers never really get over their stage fright, making every performance an ordeal. Shouldn't a point have come where performing became easy for them? But it didn't. The great Boston Celtics center Bill Russell, an all-time top ten player, vomited before every game, because every game mattered that much to him. Couldn't he just lighten up? Apparently not.

There is a combination of factors at play that make a certain thing easy for one person and hard for another. That combination includes a person's belief system, nervous system, skill set, experience level, and more. The complicated nature of personality formation that can make a person a fearless general yet afraid of spiders or a great race car driver but incapable of delivering a two-minute speech means that you may or may not be able to work effortlessly as a coach. Who knows?

But it would be good if you affirmed that maybe you will find coaching easy and affirmed that you are willing to do what it takes to make coaching easier rather than harder on you. For complicated reasons, many people do things the hardest way possible, maybe because they equate ease with taking shortcuts, not doing "enough," and acting dishonestly; maybe because they are looking for an exit strategy and have unconsciously decided to find the work impossibly hard; or maybe for some other set of reasons. See if you can sidestep such a way of thinking and affirm that you really would like coaching to be easy rather than hard.

If you do want to affirm that you would like coaching to be easy rather than hard, then all of the following would be true:

- You would hold the belief that coaching will get easier with experience.
- You would remind yourself that you are not portraying yourself as an expert but just trying to be of some help.
- You would will yourself to start working with clients, maybe in a pro bono way to begin with, so as to break through the ice of resistance and get your feet wet.
- You would adopt the strategies I've been suggesting, ones that make coaching easier rather than harder, including starting sessions calmly, easily, and with a smile, not holding on to clients' issues between sessions, et cetera.
- You would affirm that you are equal to this; that you have what it takes; that you have a reservoir of wisdom, knowledge, experience, and everything else that might be needed.
- You would focus, not on worries about potentially difficult clients or potentially rough sessions, but rather on the good feeling you have about being of some help to another human being.
- You would try not to worry.

It would be lovely if I could guarantee that you will find coaching easy. I can't. But you *may* find it easy, especially if you are inclined to *make it* easy. We can make anything harder or easier than it might otherwise be. We can hold tight, or we can surrender. We can pester ourselves or not pester ourselves. We can magnify difficulties or not magnify them. We can focus on all those troubles to come, or we can visualize success. Which will it be?

EXERCISES

Easy. Say, "Coaching is easy."

Easy. Say, "I'm not going to make coaching harder than it needs to be."

Medium. Do you have some objections to doing things the easy way? Can you sort out those objections and make some sense of them?

High bar. In your mind's eye, picture a variety of clients. See yourself helping each one of them. Some you help a lot, and some you help a little, but each is enriched by the experience. See that in your mind's eye and enjoy that feeling.

Food for Thought for Informal Coaches

What might make your informal coaching interactions easier for you? Can you give that some thought?

Writing Prompt for Self-Coaches

Write to the prompt "It would be much easier to coach myself if I…".

47

Effortless Cognitive Work

There are a number of powerful reasons why cognitive behavioral therapy is the most popular type of therapy. The top three are that it is easy to understand, easy to apply, and true to life. Who doubts that thinking as we would like to think and behaving as we would like to behave wouldn't amount to huge benefits? That just about goes without saying.

I've found it remarkably easy to work with clients in a cognitive way just by presenting one idea. All I do is invite clients to "think thoughts that serve you." I then go on to do a tiny bit of explaining: "I think you can tell I'm saying that in a very careful way. This isn't about the truth or falsity of a thought. Even true thoughts may not serve you. The criterion you want to use to judge whether to countenance a thought that's popped into your head is whether or not that thought actually serves you."

Then I'll give a simple example. If I'm working with a writer, I might say, "Say that you go onto a big online bookstore site, see the millions of books there, and think to yourself, 'Wow, there are a lot of writers out there!' That is a thought that, although abundantly true, will not serve you to think. It will demoralize you and discourage you, and three days later you may stop writing and never even know why. Why did you stop? Because three days before you let that thought 'Wow, there are a lot of writers out there!' just sit there. It would have been much better if, the instant you noticed you were having that thought, you rejected it by saying, 'Nope, sorry, that's not a thought that serves me!'"

If I'm working with a client on existential issues of meaning and purpose, my miniexplanation might sound like, "You know, many of the things we do in the service of our meaning needs don't feel meaningful as we're doing them. They may just feel like drudgery. So it may pop into our head to think, 'Wow, this doesn't feel very meaningful. Why on earth am I doing this?' You have to be very careful here, remind yourself that our efforts in the service of meaning may not always feel meaningful, and reject a thought like 'This doesn't feel very meaningful' as not serving you. Get what I mean?"

Although this is a simple idea — that we don't need to countenance thoughts that aren't serving us — it is also a tremendously important idea. And it may amount to all the cognitive work that you need to do with clients. Stopping for a moment when a client says something that you're sure isn't serving her and asking, "I wonder if what you just said is serving you?" can become one of your great secret weapons in coaching. Just that easily, you can help clients get a grip on their mind without the heavy lifting of thought blocking, thought substitution, and the other tactics of cognitive therapy.

You may be holding the idea that cognitive work is something only therapists are allowed to do. But if you think about it for a moment, I believe you'll come to the conclusion that there can't be any prohibition against a coach helping a client think thoughts that align with their dreams, goals, and intentions. How could there be such a prohibition? And why should there be one?

EXERCISES

Easy. Say, "I think I can do this sort of easy cognitive work with clients."

Easy. Say, "Yes, I would like to think thoughts that serve me."

Medium. Feel through what it would be like to do a better job of thinking only thoughts that serve you. Can you picture that?

High bar. Picture a hypothetical client scenario. Your client has just said something that you know can't be serving him very well to think. Imagine yourself asking for a moment and bringing your concern up. Can you picture yourself managing that? How might that play out?

Food for Thought for Informal Coaches

Does the sort of easy cognitive work I've described in this lesson feel out of bounds with regard to your informal coaching? Or might it have its place?

Writing Prompt for Self-Coaches

Write to the prompt "I am very aware that I often think the following true thought and that, although true, it isn't serving me..."

48

Effortless Mindfulness Work

The more self-aware clients become, the harder it is for them to repeat their mistakes, think thoughts and engage in behaviors that don't serve them, and get in their own way. That a client has become more self-aware means that he has bravely dealt with his own defensive nature, that he is not denying, rationalizing, or intellectualizing, and that he is instead seeing things more clearly, for what they are. We want this for our clients, don't we?

Nowadays, we have come to call this self-awareness "mindfulness," and so helping clients become more mindful is a customary goal. But this doesn't mean that we are asking clients to begin a meditation practice. Mindfulness has gotten associated with the practice of meditation, but the two need not be connected. You don't have to sit cross-legged to be more self-aware. Indeed, we need our self-awareness to be more portable than that, so that we can get a good grip on our mind, not just when we are on the mat, but when we are in the hurly-burly of life.

As coaches, we can think of mindfulness as simply quiet, practiced self-awareness. We can sell our clients on the idea of self-awareness, support their efforts at becoming more self-aware, and go a step further and teach them a simple mindfulness technique or two. This is easy to do, effortless really, and requires only that you learn a bit about mindfulness yourself, if you aren't much versed in it already, and that you feel comfortable bringing it up with clients.

For example, you can suggest to clients that before they do something in haste, they "take a step to the side" and give themselves a chance to pause and reflect. This step-to-the-side metaphor is an easy-to-remember and easy-to-use verbal and visual reminder of what self-awareness looks and feels like. I find that clients like this metaphor, take to it, and quickly begin to apply it in real-life situations. You can reinforce this strategy by occasionally wondering aloud, say when a client presents a tricky situation that has just occurred, "Were you able to take a step to the side before replying?" or "Were you able to take a step to the side before hitting 'send' on that email?"

With regard to mindfulness meditation, some clients will already have a meditation practice in place. However, most will not want to add a formal meditation practice to their already too-busy lives. For this majority, I teach them a simple, quick technique that marries the benefits of deep breathing with the benefits of right thinking and that amounts to a mini–mindfulness meditation. I train clients to drop a thought that serves them into a long, deep breath. The thought might be "I feel supported," "I'm completely stopping," "I make my meaning," "Right here, right now," or any other similar short phrase. This is a supersimple technique that clients tend to understand instantly and can make use of right out of the box.

Whenever you work with a client on one of her stated goals, you can introduce a little effortless mindfulness awareness by saying things like, "As you work on that, what are you going to need to be aware of?" or "What do you need to pay attention to as you work on that?" These simple reminders help clients understand that one of the quite likely unstated goals of coaching is their increased self-awareness.

EXERCISES

Easy. Say, "I can help clients increase their self-awareness."

Easy. Say, "I can help myself increase my own self-awareness."

Medium. Imagine that what you need to know is several rooms away and that between you and that knowledge is a series of locked doors. How might you unlock them?

High bar. Visualize a hypothetical client scenario. Your client has just said something that you feel reflects a significant lack of self-awareness. You could of course let the moment just slip on by; but say that you wanted to help your client gain some self-awareness, right there on the spot. What might you do? What might you say?

Food for Thought for Informal Coaches

If you wanted to pay attention to the level of self-awareness that the folks you informally coach display, how might you do that? And does that seem like something that is part of your informal coaching job description?

Writing Prompt for Self-Coaches

Write to the prompt "In order for me to gain some greater self-awareness, I think that I need to ..."

49

Effortless Support

Human beings can do with all the help they can get. We need financial support in the form of a job, physical support in the form of medical services, accounting support when it comes to our taxes, a mechanic's aid when our car breaks down, and so on. None of this typically quite tangible support is what a coach is offering her clients. She is offering what in old-fashioned parlance we might think of as "moral support," that is, the kind of support a friend, family member, or colleague might offer, the kind of support that feels like, "I'm on your side."

And what does this support sound like? Your client says, "I had a really hard time with Mike this week. I know that isn't strictly what we're working on, but can we talk about that?" You reply, "Absolutely!" That's what support sounds like. Had you replied, "No, I'm afraid we're doing X-Y-Z coaching, and that doesn't include talking about your relationships," that might be a technically appropriate response in a given set of circumstances, but your client would surely not feel supported. She would likely get back on message, as most clients want to be "good clients" — but she would probably also hold a grudge. Wouldn't you?

Effortless support is primarily a matter of saying, "Yes, absolutely!" It is an unambiguous willingness to listen, think, and try to help. That help isn't you offering to run to the store, which a friend or family member might do, or racing to watch a YouTube video because your client wants to know the difference between a natural pearl and a cultured pearl, one of a million things that a coach can't or shouldn't provide. Rather, it is you taking a certain stance, that you are on your client's side and that you are treating her as a "most favored nation," and from that position listening and responding.

That you are willing to listen doesn't mean that you are blindly willing to agree, however. It might seem that saying yes to everything your client asserts would be the path of least resistance and therefore the most effortless way to go. But even if that were so, we must bring our own thoughts, feelings, principles, and values to the table. We have that duty of care to the wider world and to our own moral imperatives. Effortless support and blind support are two different things.

This is rather like a parent saying yes to one thing after another that her child presents, until he presents something to which she must say no, maybe because it seems to her just too dangerous. She can't say yes to everything. But she can say no from the same place of care, compassion, support, and approval that the yeses have come from. She hasn't turned against her child by saying no — she may not be agreeing with him, but she is still supporting him.

If you are leaning forward, if you are nodding, if you are listening, if you are thinking about what might help, your client will know that and appreciate that. She will feel supported, which in turn will help her interact with you calmly and undefensively. It will also help her think clearly, just as you think clearly in a calm, quiet, supportive environment. Her felt sense that you are on her side will make things much easier for the two of you.

EXERCISES

Easy. Say, "I find being supportive easy."

Easy. Say, "Providing support can be effortless."

Medium. Give the following some thought: Can you support others if you don't feel sufficiently supported yourself?

High bar. Picture a hypothetical coaching scenario where your client is being a bit testy and difficult, or maybe a bit vague and unforthcoming, or maybe a bit tedious and repetitious. Can you maintain a feeling of support and an orientation of support in the scenario you're visualizing?

Food for Thought for Informal Coaches

Do you come to your informal coaching sessions more with a desire to get something fixed or a desire to be supportive?

Writing Prompt for Self-Coaches

Write to the prompt "I don't find it easy to support myself because..."

50

Effortless Accountability

There are many easy, or relatively easy, ways that you can help clients hold themselves accountable as they try to meet their goals and achieve their dreams. Here are several.

One way that makes extra work for you but that is valuable for clients is the client check-in. You might say to a client, "I'd love to have you check in with me, if you feel like doing that. That's for your sake, not for mine. Would you like to do that? And if so, how often — every day, once a week, as the need arises, or…?" Even if clients do not check in according to the schedule they name, they will be thinking about checking in, which means that they will at least be keeping their goals and intentions in mind.

A second way that makes extra work for you but that clients find heartwarming and lovely is you checking in with them. Say that you're aware your client has some difficult thing happening on Tuesday, perhaps a hard conversation at work. You might drop him an email late on that day and inquire, "How did that conversation go?" Naturally, you would only check in judiciously, as there are many situations where your client would prefer not to hear from you. But the occasional check-in from you can be a rather beautiful thing, as it reminds him that you are out there, thinking of him, which in turn promotes his self-accountability.

A third way is to begin sessions with a careful focus on what has and hasn't transpired between the last session and this one. This might sound like, "Let's begin by checking in on the things you'd intended to get done. How did those go?" Of course, this inquiry may make your client feel uncomfortable and embarrassed, if he hasn't got good news to report. But it is nevertheless right, proper, and valuable that you monitor your cocreated goals. And because your client knows that this question is coming, he may well get a lot of work done at the last minute on the day of your session, just so that he can report some good news.

A fourth way is to use the activity of summarizing at the end of session as a way to help clients hold themselves accountable to themselves. This might sound like some variation of "Okay, I think you've named some clear intentions for the next month. If I've got it right, it's to exercise every day for half an hour, get your taxes untangled, and visit jewelry websites to see how you might like to set up your own jewelry website. Have I got that right?"

A fifth way is to pause for a moment when a client says that she would like to get a certain thing done so as to ask for her buy-in. This might sound like, "Let's stop for a second there. So you'd like to set up a crowdfunding campaign for your documentary film? Do you feel like committing to that?" Your client will likely nod and agree, at which point you can move right on to envisioning the work involved and getting further commitments from your client — for instance, the commitment to compare crowdfunding sites and the commitment to create a synopsis of her documentary film.

Although some of these techniques do make work for you, they are nevertheless easy, or relatively easy. They are certainly valuable for your clients. And who knows, you may find your own, even easier ways of helping clients hold themselves accountable.

EXERCISES

Easy. Say, "It is good to help clients hold themselves accountable."

Easy. Say, "I provide support and accountability."

Medium. What does the phrase "helping clients hold themselves accountable to themselves" conjure for you?

High bar. Imagine a hypothetical client scenario where your client has been dodging committing to any specific goals. Each time the two of you come near to landing on something he might commit to, he presents a reason why that wouldn't work or wouldn't be right at this time. What do you think you might try so as to pin him down a bit and help him commit? And how might you build accountability into what you try?

Food for Thought for Informal Coaches

Do you offer the folks you informally coach some way of holding themselves accountable? If you currently don't, do you think you might like to add that to the way you coach?

Writing Prompt for Self-Coaches

Write to the prompt "I think that I would like to hold myself accountable in the following ways…"

51

Calling for a Moment

A time may come in session when it makes good sense to say, "I wonder, can we stop for a moment and take a look at that?" It takes a bit of practice to arrive at a place where you feel comfortable gently but energetically stopping your client's flow, but that's an important habit to acquire. If you don't acquire that habit, many chances to deepen the relationship or to be of some help will pass the two of you on by.

There are many possible reasons for making that "let's stop for a moment" call.

It might be that your client has just brought up some painful historical material and now is determined to rush on past it; and you decide that you want to take a moment to acknowledge what she has just shared. Stopping here might sound like, "I wonder if we can just take a moment." Stopping in this way is likely what your client needs but can't quite ask for herself. She would like to know that she has been heard — and you can show that you've heard her by asking for a moment.

It might be that your client has brought up some recent success but — maybe because it seems too small to applaud, maybe so as not to seem prideful, or maybe because they haven't noticed that it *was* a success — they haven't acknowledged it as a success. Stopping here might sound like, "Whoa, let's stop for a moment and celebrate that. That wasn't so easy to get done. Congrats on doing that!" Not only will your stopping like that please them, but it will help them better understand what success looks like and that they are, in fact, achieving successes.

It might be that your client has been chatting about some challenging issue and has just let drop what you take to be an important clue — some telling experience in school, some ongoing conflict with a sibling, some chronic health problem. Stopping here might sound like, "Hold on a second. That sounded important. Can we spend a moment there?" If your client agrees to stop there for a moment, all you need to say next is "Tell me a little bit more about that."

It might be that your client has just covered a lot of ground and you have the sense that without a bit of summarizing the two of you are about to get overwhelmed. Stopping here might sound like, "Jane, let's stop for a second. I need to summarize a bit for myself so that I don't lose track." Your client won't argue with that, as she too will understand that a lot just got said. You don't need to worry about producing some sort of perfect summary — just do your best to share what you see as a few headlines from what just transpired. Your client will appreciate your effort, and it will also give her a chance to catch her breath.

Calling for a moment is a rather important coaching tactic. Anything that you might want to do in session to help a client, from commenting to commiserating to making a suggestion to asking a quality question, can happen only if you believe that you have permission to speak up and if you can find the courage to speak up. This may prove a stretch for you at the beginning of your coaching career, but it is one of those things that can become effortless with practice and experience. You will get used to saying, "Can we stop there for a moment?" and your clients will get used to hearing you say that — and they will welcome that thoughtful consideration.

Easy. Say, "I can call for a moment."

Easy. Say, "I can interrupt my client's flow if I feel there's a good reason to do so."

Medium. Do you see interrupting as rude or even as dangerous? Can you tease apart your thoughts and feelings and see if you might arrive at a new willingness to stop sessions when necessary?

High bar. Picture a hypothetical client session. Your client has just said something that really ought not be allowed to just zip on by. Picture yourself saying your version of "Whoa, I wonder if we can stop there for just a moment?" What will your way of saying that be?

Food for Thought for Informal Coaches

Picture yourself doing a little informal coaching with a family member. Can you imagine a style of interrupting where the other person doesn't feel like he or she is being shut down or criticized?

Writing Prompt for Self-Coaches

Write to the prompt "If I find myself telling myself the same old story about something, I think that I can call for a moment by..."

52

When a Client Says This

Clients will sometimes say things that are meant to provoke us, set us back on our heels a bit, take our eye off noticing that they aren't doing their work, amount to a complaint, or serve some other agenda. These are testing moments, and a coach will want to have her practiced ways of reacting to these minitests, including by internally smiling and by whispering to herself, "No need to get defensive here. Be easy."

Here are five typical client announcements. As you read, imagine how it would feel to be on the receiving end of each.

Scenario 1

Client: "I must be the worst client ever!"

This may mean, "I am very proud of being so difficult!" Or it may mean, "I'm so embarrassed to be making things so hard for you!" Or it may mean, "I am very frustrated, and I think I should stop with this coaching."

How you might respond, maybe with a slight chuckle: "Everybody has difficulty getting things done and reaching their goals. Maybe we need to recalibrate our goals a bit? Should we take a look at that?"

Scenario 2

Client: "Have you ever seen this before?"

This may mean, "Aren't my problems quite special and unique?" Or it may mean, "Do you have much experience with this sort of thing?" Or it may mean, "I am in too deep a hole to ever get out of it."

How you might respond, maybe with a warm smile: "I've seen lots of folks and lots of difficulties. Let's dive a little deeper into what's going on here."

Scenario 3

Client: "I don't think you're understanding me at all."

This may mean exactly what it sounds like it means. Or it may mean, "I am going to keep switching from one thing to another to keep us both off-balance." Or it may mean, "No one has ever understood me in the slightest."

How you might respond, maybe with a bit of an apologetic air: "Oh, I'm so sorry! Let's give it another go, shall we?"

Scenario 4

Client: "I feel like you're pressuring me."

This may mean exactly what it sounds like it means, as, maybe out of frustration, you may indeed be pressing your client to get some work done and some goals achieved. Or it may mean, "Yes, I haven't been doing what I claimed I would do, but I don't need you to keep reminding me of that!"

How you might respond, maybe quite gravely: "I'm really sorry. Definitely, let's reduce the temperature. Let's just take a moment and see where we might want to go next, someplace far away from pressure."

Scenario 5

Client: "I don't think we're making any progress."

This may mean exactly what it sounds like it means, that your client is frustrated by her lack of progress, but it may not be clear whether she is calling herself out or is pointing a finger at you. It may be the one, the other, or — quite likely, as you are in this together — both.

How you might respond, maybe as a soft-spoken teacher would: "It might be good if we focused on daily practice rather than on progress. Progress is a tricky idea and not always the best way to measure things. Can we circle back around to the idea of daily practice?"

No one likes being tested, confronted, or played in these ways. But if you intend to help people, you must get used to dealing with people. They will come with defenses, games, complaints, and agendas. Over time, this is a place to become an accomplished artist, an artist at human interactions. There may not be a higher artistry in the universe, including the high artistries of theoretical physics, frescoes, and symphonies. Enjoy this learning, even if it is sometimes painful.

EXERCISES

Easy. Say, "I can weather clients' pushback, criticism, and agendas."

Easy. Say, "I don't have to respond defensively, even if I feel attacked."

Medium. Interactions of the sort that I described above, or just the specter of such interactions happening, can turn a coach off coaching. Check in with yourself to make sure that you won't give up on coaching just because some sessions prove rough and testing.

High bar. Imagine that you've been pressuring a client a bit, maybe to state a clear goal, maybe to recommit to a previously stated goal, maybe to try harder. Suddenly your client exclaims, "You're really pressuring me!" Picture yourself not tightening up and not getting defensive and maybe even growing easy. From this place of ease, how would you like to respond? What might you say?

Food for Thought for Informal Coaches

How do you react when a person you're informally coaching pushes back? Are you happy with the way you react? Would you like to begin reacting differently?

Writing Prompt for Self-Coaches

Write to the prompt "I know that I play certain games with myself. Here's one that I would like to change…"

53

Big Dreams, Small Steps

Not all of our clients have big dreams. But many do. And even something that doesn't quite sound like a big dream, like getting better organized, playing some recognizable tunes on the piano, or dealing with a recently deceased parent's estate, may still amount to a lot of real work. Just about anything a client wishes to accomplish, from finding inner peace to advancing at their job, is bound to amount to real work. And if there is also a big dream involved, like winning a Pulitzer or the Nobel Prize...

Whether a big dream is on the table or just something that amounts to real work, the only way for a human being to logically and effectively proceed is to take the small, regular steps that are right in front of him. You can't leap from here to the Nobel Prize or from here to getting your garage straightened out. There is no leap to be made; there are only small steps to take. And not just any old small steps, but the most effective and productive ones.

There is a real difference between any old small steps and small steps in the service of that dream. Say that your client's band is getting known locally, but he needs something (in addition to pure luck) to propel it to the next level. He could set a goal of writing to a famous musician who happens to be a friend of a friend and asking him if the band could play for him and get some advice. Or he could set a goal of uploading the band's latest tune to the internet. Each of these small steps would take only a few minutes to accomplish, but the potential for impact is vastly different. Which is the bigger small step?

Most folks find it hard to do the latter but find it almost impossible to do the former, even though it is clear that the former has the potential for the greater payoff. Not all small steps are created equal. So rather than saying, "What small steps would you like to take this coming week?" which perhaps gives a client too much permission to pick the smallest steps possible, you might say instead, "Of the many small steps you might take this week, which ones seem the most useful to take?" This way of framing the question helps a client distinguish among his possible steps and presses him to pick the best small steps at his disposal.

At the same time, we cheerlead for the dream. This might sound like, "Great that you intend to get to the poetry every day this week! By the way, you also mentioned a competition you were thinking of entering? Catch me up on that a bit." Or "Lovely that you're enjoying doing some singing every day! By the way, I think you were intending to sing two songs at your daughter's wedding? Catch me up on that a bit." Or "Excellent that you got some of those hard parts done on your website! By the way, I think you were going to try to launch your business at the end of next month? Catch me up on that a bit."

A client wants to get something extraordinary or something quite ordinary done. We can help by keeping a careful eye on the many steps required.

EXERCISES

Easy. Say, "Dreams and small steps, not the one or the other but both."

Easy. Play with the phrases "reality testing" and "dream upholding" and see if the phrase "I can reality test with clients while upholding their dreams" resonates for you.

Medium. How do your clients' aspirations affect you? Are you happy when you hear from a client that he or she is harboring some big dream, or does that feel like it puts extra pressure on you?

High bar. Picture a hypothetical scenario where your new client is articulating a very big dream — say, to become a star in his field — but he sounds rather resistant to doing the sorts of things you presume he ought to be doing in order to make that dream come true. How does that make you feel? Annoyed? Resentful? Doubtful? Ready to roll up your sleeves? How might you proceed?

Food for Thought for Informal Coaches

Do you have a different approach when you are coaching someone with a big dream (say, to get into an Ivy League college) versus someone who isn't announcing any such dream? Do you have the sense that you work differently or feel differently in these two situations?

Writing Prompt for Self-Coaches

Write to the prompt "I do indeed have a dream. And these are my next steps..."

54

The Art of Prioritizing

One of the ways that you are trying to be of a little help is by directing your client to focus on what is more important to him, rather than on what is less important to him. You might think that folks wouldn't need that sort of aid, as obviously they would be prioritizing their life in exactly that way on their own. But of course we know better. The majority of people regularly fill up their day with thoughts, feelings, and activities that do not match their vision of what's important. They need help prioritizing, and we can provide that help.

In practice, this can sound as simple as "What two or three important things do you want to attend to this coming week?" Let's say that our client replies, "I want to focus on improving my health, working on my research paper, and decluttering my office." A good next question from us is, "What does that look like?" This invites our client to become more concrete. To this question, our client might reply, "Well, I want to get to the gym three times this week, write five days this week, and maybe tackle decluttering the office at least for a few hours one day."

So far, so good. Our client has now named the actions and behaviors that align with his intentions. But he hasn't yet ordered them or prioritized them in a temporal way. We don't yet have a picture of where in the day these things will happen. So that would be a quality question to ask next. That might sound like, "Okay, why don't you paint me a picture of your days. What will come before what? How will that all work?"

Your client may well get stuck here, as most people aren't used to organizing their life and their days this carefully or this consciously. He will likely shake his head and say, "I'm not exactly sure." To which we can make the following sort of reply: "Okay, tell me what Monday might look like." Then we provide some quality quiet as he gets Monday in his mind's eye and tries to picture that reality.

His attempt to get his head around what Monday could look like is likely to get him into a funk, as he realizes that his Monday is already "full of stuff," leaving little or no room for the gym, his research paper, or the decluttering. This is an important moment in the coaching, because our client can get demoralized as he faces something that he has of course already known, if only subconsciously: that his life, as he is living it, is not permitting him to get to the important things. We are ready for our client sinking a bit here, and so we stand prepared to cheerlead for hope and possibility.

Our client may well say, "Monday just doesn't look possible." Rather than replying, "Well, how does Tuesday look?" (which will prove further demoralizing, as Tuesday is going to look just as unavailable as Monday did), we might wonder aloud, "Let's look very carefully at Monday and see what might be possible. Run me through Monday slowly." We then get into the weeds of Monday, which is exactly where we need to be, because it is in the weeds that we can begin to talk about specific changes our client might want to make.

At the end of a chat of this sort, it's quite likely that our client's days — and life — will be prioritized rather differently, much more in keeping with how he actually wants to live.

EXERCISES

Easy. Say, "I can help my clients prioritize."

Easy. Feel through whether helping clients prioritize feels right or pushy.

Medium. If you currently don't do a great job of prioritizing in your own life, what one or two changes might you make to help you live your life in a more mindful way?

High bar. Picture a hypothetical client session. You have the sense that your client is getting frustrated because she isn't coming close to achieving any of her stated goals. It strikes you that helping her prioritize might be a very useful next step. How would you introduce the matter? Picture such a session, picture your client speaking, and picture yourself asking for a moment. How might your effort to help your client begin to prioritize play itself out?

Food for Thought for Informal Coaches

In your current informal coaching, do you typically help the folks you are coaching prioritize their efforts in a "this might come first, this might come second, this might come third" sort of way? If not, might it make sense to include that helping tactic in your approach?

Writing Prompt for Self-Coaches

Write to the prompt "I think that I do a rather poor job of prioritizing because…"

55

Cheerleading for Action

A therapist might be happy and pleased to say at the end of a session, "I think you learned something today." For a coach, that isn't quite enough. Insight is important and wonderful, and we want our clients to gain clarity, better understand their own motivations, increase their self-awareness, and learn about themselves. But human nature being what it is, insight doesn't equal change or growth and doesn't amount to enough help. A client who gains insight is not aided nearly as much as a client who gains insight and then takes action based on that insight.

Therapy can proceed — and regularly does proceed — whether or not a client "does anything." Coaching can't really. Coaching is premised on the idea that your client will do something. That is why your client has come to you; it is a centerpiece of the agreement between you. If, say, you're a business coach and one of your client's goals is to build his self-confidence, then you would want him to do things at work aligned with nurturing a more confident him. He wants that, you want that for him, and if he isn't reporting that he has finally managed to ask for a raise or has finally refused those extra last-minute assignments, you would know to continue to cheerlead for him to take those courageous actions.

Human beings are regularly eager to announce that they are "feeling really good" about having arrived at some insight, which can be their way of saying, "And can we maybe not talk about the next steps, all the work involved in turning that insight into something tangible?" Our job is to smile, congratulate them on their new insight, and then move directly on to "And what actions align with that insight? What do you intend to do?" Our client may well sigh — and then walk through the door that we've opened, willing himself to picture all those difficult but necessary next actions.

To cheerlead for action doesn't mean that you must cheerlead only for large actions. Inviting a client who wants to return to the symphony she's been writing and who's put it aside for two years might sound like, "What makes sense, given your real life? Maybe twenty minutes a day of writing?" If you were to try to lobby or cheerlead for two hours of writing a day or some other ambitious and likely unrealistic goal, your client might agree just to be accommodating, but she probably wouldn't come close to doing *any* writing. Often the right-sized action is small and not gigantic.

It is good to have every session end with your client having a very clear picture of the actions she has agreed to take between now and her next session. You can summarize those for your client, or you can invite her to summarize. Once they've been summarized, you can then cheerlead a little by saying, "Okay! I look forward to hearing how that went!" or "Okay! I look forward to your check-ins!" This simple routine of summarizing and cheerleading ends sessions on a positive, energetic note and primes clients to get to work.

EXERCISES

Easy. Say, "I can cheerlead for action."

Easy. Say, "I believe in effort."

Medium. If you aren't wonderful at cheerleading for action in your own life, consider why that might be so — and what you might like to do to make a change in the direction of self-efficacy. If you do arrive at some insight, follow it up with an action plan and cheer-lead for the actions you just identified.

High bar. Picture a hypothetical client scenario. You and your client are having a useful conversation about some issue, and you have the sense that some movement has occurred and some insight has been gained. Feel through what it's like to move from the comfort of that easy chatting to the prickliness of a next conversation that begins with a question like, "And what would you like to do?" Picture yourself equal to making that movement and easy with making that movement.

Food for Thought for Informal Coaches

Get an informal coaching session in your mind's eye. Picture the session concluding and the person you're coaching not having a clear idea of what action she is supposed to take next. Then imagine the session ending with her having a very clear idea of what action she is supposed to take next. Aren't those dramatically different outcomes?

Writing Prompt for Self-Coaches

Write to the prompt "I know there is a certain action I ought to take in my life. I think I can face taking that action if I..."

56

The Discomfort of Limited Progress

Stated goals in coaching sound like, "I want to improve my health" or "I want to get my novel written" or "I want to move my career forward." But virtually every client will also be harboring the unstated goal of "I want to make measurable progress." They will be holding this unstated goal for three reasons: that *progress* is the word we use to measure getting things done, and getting things done seems important, and it has been drilled into our heads that making progress is a stand-alone value or virtue.

When we say of someone, "He's not making progress," we are not applauding him for paying beautiful attention to process. We are criticizing him. That is the Western or American way. Transcendentalist philosophers like Ralph Waldo Emerson and Henry David Thoreau exalted progress, loved the image of the upward spiral, and believed that the species was moving forward and upward toward a full manifestation of what they believed to be inherent human goodness. Those beliefs paralleled then-newfangled ideas about evolution and the upward spiral of humans from apes.

If I were to want to play the same musical note every day, simply because I found it beautiful and soothing, rather than learn to play a sonata or a concerto, part of me would not be satisfied, because we have baked into us the idea that more is better, that bigger is better, that a moment of joy as we make a thing does not count the way that finishing that thing does. To say it another way, we have elevated product and progress a mile higher than process, making it that much harder for us to enjoy any given moment or appreciate the process side of life.

So, as coaches, we must deal with the way in which not making progress disturbs and demoralizes clients. Not one in a million clients will say, "I had a great week because I ate a delicious peach on Monday and some marvelous grapes on Tuesday" if what they had intended to do, and didn't do, was work on their business plan. Nor can a coach say, "Yes, you didn't work on your business plan this week, but did you by any chance eat a delicious peach?" Both coach and client are in the progress game, and we are indeed obliged to try to help clients make progress. At the same time, we don't have to get hooked into the idea that only progress counts.

Say that a client begins a session by confessing, "I didn't work on developing my invention this week." Internally, we can think, "Oh, no!" or we can think, "Okay." To think, "Oh, no!" reflects our own baked-in belief that no progress equals failure. By calmly saying, "Okay" internally, we are dialing down the drama, refusing to judge or criticize, and reducing our client's bad feelings about himself. This puts us both in a better position to chat about next steps and renewed commitments.

Yes, we want our clients to make progress, and we want to help them make progress. But we also want them to breathe and live. We want them to find a measure of happiness in daily experiences that do not look anything like progress. We can attend to the idea of progress as a valuable thing without exalting progress and without making it the best measure or the only measure of what help looks like. Progress is important, but it is not everything.

If we take that wider-angle view — that progress is one measure but not the only measure — we will by our very energy and outlook help clients feel less frustrated and less down on themselves when, during a given period, they haven't made progress. Yes, just as they do, we want our clients to make progress. But we also want them to feel deeply okay even if, between when we saw them last and seeing them now, they didn't lose those three pounds or write those two thousand words. Progress is not the only goal and not the only measure.

EXERCISES

Easy. Say, "Progress is important but not everything."

Easy. Say, "I can help clients navigate a felt lack of progress."

Medium. Consider the following question: "What actually helps me make progress?"

High bar. Picture a hypothetical client scenario where for several sessions your client has failed to make any progress getting her website built, which is holding her whole business plan hostage. How might you help her simultaneously forgive herself or be easier with that lack of progress while at the same time supporting her intention to get her website built? What might that feel like and look like?

Food for Thought for Informal Coaches

When you informally coach folks, what measures of success do you have in mind in addition to making progress?

Writing Prompt for Self-Coaches

Write to the prompt "My own complicated relationship to progress looks like…"

57

When Life Intervenes

Occasionally a client will do his work week in and week out without life intervening much. He'll work on writing his family history every day, he'll practice his Greek three times a week, he'll get to tai chi classes regularly, and so on. But that is really so rare! For most people, life has a way of sharply and rudely intervening: your client's father suddenly gets sick; your client's water heater breaks; the in-laws visit; tax time arrives; a week of vacation, as lovely as that may be, throws him completely off his routine.

These events do not make our clients happy. Our client may shrug, sigh, and say, "It is what it is," accepting the reality and inevitability of disruption, but this reality doesn't please him much. What pleases him even less is how hard he has found it to return to his hard-won routine. The in-laws leave, but your client doesn't recommence writing his family history. The water heater gets fixed, but somehow that event has cost him his motivation to get to the tai chi class. He finds himself shaking his head: "What's going on? Did that disruption cause me to lose everything?"

Picture a bar of iron and a blacksmith's furnace. The iron is iron before it enters the forge — it is as hard as, well, iron. The blacksmith introduces it into the furnace, heats it at a high temperature, and then can work the iron — until it cools. Then it is iron again. He must return it to the forge before he can shape it once more. The hard work our client is trying to do — and it is experienced as hard work, or he would have done it with a snap of his fingers and without having hired a coach — is like that bar of iron. It was hard; it grew pliable in the furnace of routine, care, motivation, and structure that the coaching has provided; and, life having intervened, it cooled and hardened. It is iron again — and you know what that means.

We need to understand that life intervening is typically no small matter — it is the equivalent of an iron bar cooling and becoming unworkable — and we may well want to communicate that understanding to our client even before the interruption occurs. This might sound like, "Okay, your in-laws will be visiting for two weeks. That is a long time! Describe to me how you'll keep your routine going while they're around — even if it's just a reduced version of your routine. Because if you can't manage to keep it up at least a little, that may have a cost after they leave. That sort of disruption can knock things for a loop! So let's plan for that and keep your routine going while the in-laws are around, if that's at all possible."

One of the reasons we rightly shy away from the idea of measuring the effectiveness of our work with clients in terms of progress is precisely because when life intervenes, the train may leave the tracks, and our work will likely be to deal with that derailment. A train zipping along may be making progress. But is that what we would want to call getting a battered locomotive back on its wheels and able to limp to the next station? We may have helped save the day, but the phrase "making progress" doesn't capture that dynamic.

Expect that life will intervene and make it hard for your clients; and expect that a good deal of your work with clients will have to do with dealing with the consequences of those interruptions and derailments. That is important work; and thank goodness that we are there to help!

EXERCISES

Easy. Say, "It is likely that my clients will have a rocky time of it at some points."

Easy. Say, "I can help my clients weather life's disruptions."

Medium. Remember a time when you were going about your business pretty well and life seriously intervened. Feel through the magnitude of that disruption. Does that give you a better sense of the sorts of earthquakes with which your clients are likely to have to contend?

High bar. Picture a hypothetical client scenario. Your client has just let drop that something rather big and disruptive is about to happen — say, that she and her husband are about to engage in a three-month remodel of their house. Picture yourself warning her about how disruptive to her routine that is likely to prove. What might you say?

Food for Thought for Informal Coaches

You come to a meeting with someone you're informally coaching and learn that something large and unexpected has happened in her life since the last time the two of you met. How would you like to react to that news?

Writing Prompt for Self-Coaches

Write to the prompt "When life intervenes, I think that a good plan will be..."

58

When Personality Intervenes

Personality regularly prevents progress. If you write a good novel that could be better, and a literary agent who looks at it explains how it could be better, and you thumb your nose at her and exclaim, "Absolutely not!" and as a result your novel is never published and you end up in some other walk of life, that was your personality preventing you from making progress as a novelist. Wars, plagues, and tidal waves didn't intervene. You got in your own way.

Or maybe you have a big success as an actor and now have easy access to all the drugs and sex a person could possibly want, and you avail yourself of all of that, and you become a wreck, and you get a wonderful next role but come onto the set drunk and high every day and have to be replaced by another actor. That was you preventing yourself from making progress as an actor. You had that one in a million chance to have a great career and squandered it, and of course you can and probably will point the finger and blame others and make your case for how the world has failed you, but that was you.

Or maybe your band miraculously rises above the noise of so many acts and becomes well known, and now each band member suddenly has all sorts of grievances, about who should be writing the music, about who should have gotten more credit for your hit single, about who should stand a few inches in front of everyone else because your fans love them the most. This bickering goes on for a month, even while your manager is orchestrating a grand tour, and as the tour is about to launch none of you can stand being in the same room with the others, and the band breaks up, and that's that. That was personality at work.

Even a client who genuinely wants to make progress, however he or she defines progress, wants to stubbornly express his or her personality more. There is a powerful sense in which clients feel that they must be true to themselves, even if that sabotages their efforts and prevents them from making progress. In the simplest instance, it will sound like a client saying, after the two of you have agreed that there are five wonderful reasons why he ought to write first thing in the morning, before his day job starts: "But I'm a night person." As if a "night person" can't wake up early and write! This is how personality plays itself out in session.

Because personality plays itself out in these ways, you don't want to attach too much to the idea of client progress, as you are dealing with an adamantine, rock-hard thing. Do not feel that you need to press or force. Instead, you can be soft, subtle, and gentle. You can say, for example, "Do you think you might be able to give morning writing a try for a week? Just as a tiny experiment? We don't need to have a lot of hope of it working — but maybe it's worth a try?" This way of speaking may allow you to enlist your client's freedom to be the person he would like to be, that part of him not gobbled up and held hostage by his formed personality.

EXERCISES

Easy. Say, "Clients will come with a personality. They can't help themselves in that regard."

Easy. Say, "Given the power of personality to block the way, I am not attached to the idea of client progress."

Medium. Pick a feature of your own personality that you know doesn't serve you all that well. See if you can come up with one or two suggestions as to how you might like to bring about a personality upgrade.

High bar. Go a step further and actually make one or two of those changes. Notice your resistance and the many and varied ways you explain to yourself why that change isn't really possible. Won't clients be doing exactly the same thing? And isn't a rich part of your job description to figure out how you can be of some help even in the face of rock-hard personality?

Food for Thought for Informal Coaches

Picture a situation where you have the intuition that what you are about to suggest to someone you're informally coaching isn't really a match for his or her personality. How might you reframe, soften, or otherwise change your suggestion so as to ensure it is heard and received?

Writing Prompt for Self-Coaches

Write to the prompt "I suspect that my own personality gets in the way of me making progress in the following ways..."

59

Practice, Process, and Purpose

We would love it if our clients made progress, and our clients would love that, too. But there are another three *p* words that are at least as important as *progress*: namely, *practice*, *process*, and *purpose*. The four together amount to a rather beautiful and complete coaching agenda.

It is good if we invite our clients to understand the value of regular practice, the varieties of practice available to them, and how just about anything important to them can be conceptualized as a regular (or, better yet, daily) practice. We also would like clients to understand how many obstacles to regular practice they are likely to encounter — from their environment, from those around them, from ambient anxiety, and from their own personality makeup. If a coach is inclined to teach, there is a lot of excellent teaching that can take place in this lane.

For instance, maybe your client has a number of health agenda items: she wants to walk every day, lose twenty pounds, find a new physical therapist, reduce her stress through mindfulness meditation, et cetera. It would be useful and rather easy for a coach to say something like, "I wonder if we can combine some of these activities into a daily health practice? Maybe, say, you set aside ninety minutes every day to meditate and walk, followed by meal planning for that day? Something along those lines?" Presenting your client with that sort of picture will help her better understand how she might bundle her activities in a way that makes them more achievable.

Another important *p* word is *process*. Much of what we do in life demands that we let go of the idea we can impose our will on people, events, or situations and that we instead focus our attention on natural and inevitable processes — like, for example, the creative process. You can't make a masterpiece happen: you can only show up, do your creative work, and see if the result pleases you. Some large percentage won't please you, and some small (but hopefully significant) percentage will. That's the truth about the creative process.

If you need each one of the songs that you write to be a masterpiece, or if you stop writing songs because your first few aren't any good, that is you either intentionally or unintentionally misunderstanding the creative process. This process comes with mistakes, messes, failures, uninspired work, ordinary work, and all the rest. It is important that as coaches we help our clients face these realities, whatever the specific process may be that connects to the goal they've set for themselves.

The last important *p* word is *purpose*. To my mind, it's important for clients to identify what's important to them in life and to think of those important things as their life purpose choices, their highest-bar intentions. This way of looking at purpose shifts it from the traditional "searching for the purpose of life" view to what I believe to be a truer and more useful view: that there is no singular purpose to life and that we are obliged to make our own life-purpose choices on an ongoing basis.

Whatever your own position on purpose may be, it is a significant coaching issue, as clients who experience a lack of purpose in life may be able to go through the motions in life and may even get a lot of things done, but they will be rather unlikely to achieve the goals they set for themselves. How can you write a gardening book, build a business, run a marathon, or do anything else that requires sustained effort if you lack purpose?

All four of these *p*'s are extremely important. Progress, practice, process, and purpose: doesn't that make for a rather lovely mantra?

Easy. Say, "I pay attention to progress, practice, process, and purpose."

Easy. Do one of these four need some further thinking on your part? If so, carve out a little time to do that thinking.

Medium. Process is a rich and also a rather complicated concept. Try describing it in your own words. What, for example, does the phrase "honoring the process" mean to you?

High bar. In your mind's eye, visualize a hypothetical client scenario. Your client has presented you with a number of goals and intentions, and you have the sense that she could logically bundle some of these into a regular practice or even a daily practice. Picture yourself asking for a moment and explaining what that bundling might look like.

Food for Thought for Informal Coaches

Consider your informal coaching work. Do you typically touch base on all four of the *p*'s when you coach? Are there one or more that you'd like to begin checking in on more regularly?

Writing Prompt for Self-Coaches

Write to the prompt "Of these four — progress, practice, process, and purpose — the one that interests me the most at the moment is..."

60

Hope and Forgiveness

We would like clients to make progress where it makes sense to consider progress the appropriate goal. We would also like clients to relax about making progress where progress isn't the appropriate goal and where, for instance, process rather than progress is the more relevant concept.

For instance, if a client is avoiding finishing writing her TV pilot because she is afraid that it will be criticized once folks take a look at it, there we want her to manage that anxiety, get to the end of her script, and make that sort of progress. But if she can't end her TV pilot because the ending hasn't quite come to her yet, there we are more in the territory of process than progress, and we don't want her pestering herself about a lack of progress. Forcing an ending might have the look of making progress, but at the cost of ending her script poorly.

You can tell that this is a subtle business, because how is a coach to know for sure, or really at all, whether a client is stalled because she is anxious about her script's reception or stalled because the script's ending hasn't come to her yet? Well, a coach can ask. In this particular set of circumstances, a quality question might sound like, "Do you think you've stopped making progress for some technical reason, like not knowing how the story is supposed to end, or for some psychological reason, like being worried about what people will think of the pilot?" That would be a useful question!

You might even begin to offer clients a version of the serenity prayer: "Grant me the serenity to accept process when I'm engaged in process, the courage to make progress when I can make progress, and the wisdom to know when I should be thinking 'process' and when I should be thinking 'progress.'" Whether your client is trying to build up his product sales, recover from an injury, plan for an active retirement, or direct a multi-million-dollar film, he would benefit greatly from keeping his eye on this distinction and embracing this wisdom.

If a client is engaged in the sort of thing where progress is the right concept and if he or she is failing to make sufficient progress, then we can do three related things: suggest to them that they deeply forgive themselves for not making the progress that they had hoped to make; help them remain hopeful that they can and will make progress; and invite them to get back on the horse, reannounce their intentions, and restate their commitments.

The simple three-part plan to present is comprised of self-forgiveness, hope, and renewed effort. This might sound like, "May was a very hard month. Try to forgive yourself for not making much progress on your website, and let's affirm that June will be much better. What would you like to get done in June? Paint me a picture." This way of speaking provides both support and accountability, as it puts May in your client's rearview mirror and focuses her on an active, productive, much better June.

EXERCISES

Easy. Say, "I want clients to feel hopeful."

Easy. Say, "I want clients not to beat themselves up."

Medium. Is it your mindset that clients need to earn self-forgiveness by getting their work done, whatever that work may be, or can they just forgive themselves without doing anything? Ponder your position on this fundamental question.

High bar. Get a hypothetical client scenario in mind. Picture a client who is quite down on herself because she is getting very little done and doesn't feel very motivated to do much. What might you say to help her do the three things I described above: forgive herself, feel some renewed hope, and recommit to her goals? What might your pitch sound like?

Food for Thought for Informal Coaches

It may well be that encouraging self-forgiveness does not feel like something you ought to be doing when you informally coach. That may feel a bit inappropriate or out-of-bounds. What are your thoughts on whether or not you have permission to invite the folks you informally coach to practice self-forgiveness?

Writing Prompt for Self-Coaches

Write to the question "Must I earn self-forgiveness, or can I just forgive myself?"

61

What Clients Bring

Clients are not some fabulous blank slate. They come with a formed personality, a history of experiences, small and large anxieties, and all sorts of grudges, regrets, and disappointments. All of this will color what they are inclined to do, willing to do, and capable of doing. You do not need to hunt for some too simple, overarching, and essentially pejorative label for who they are, some label like "borderline personality" or "obsessive-compulsive personality." Just think "human being." That's who's coming through the door, a human being, and that's what they will bring, everything human.

They will bring a history. Whether or not you want to know much about that history or need to know much about it connects to your style of working and to the particulars of the situation. Sometimes I find that I need to know very little about a client's past, as we jump right into working on the present and the future. Other times, the past is very present. But whether it is in the background or the foreground, your client's history is always there. You can turn to it, as you might turn to a reference book, to help you and your client better understand what's going on.

They will also bring anxiety. Anxiety is a feature of our warning system alerting us to danger, and as such it is a natural, integral, and inevitable part of living. A lot of coaching has to do with normalizing client anxiety and helping clients do things even if they are feeling anxious. If human beings did things only when they weren't feeling anxious, actors wouldn't audition, musicians wouldn't perform, law school graduates wouldn't take the bar exam, and surgical interns wouldn't make it through their first day of grand rounds. A significant part of a coach's linguistic repertoire is her being able to say, "Yes, of course that may make you anxious, but…"

Clients also bring undeniable strengths and resources. It is all too easy to picture clients as "less than" just by virtue of them needing coaching. But you may be working with clients smart enough to win a Nobel Prize in physics, strong enough to climb the Himalayas, resourceful enough to work a taxing job and raise children single-handedly, brave enough to serve as a firefighter or a trauma nurse, and resilient enough to have survived parental bullying and other abuse. Give your clients credit where credit is due and even a little more credit than that, for all the unseen and unacknowledged ways in which they have proved strong and resourceful.

This is all by way of saying that when you work with a client, you are working with a person. You aren't working with a specimen, as if you had an insect under a microscope, or with a label, as if a human being were the equivalent of something called PTSD or OCD or ADHD.

You are working with a member of your species, someone exactly as complicated as you are. You may be working with a client *on* a goal or an array of goals, but you are more fundamentally working *with* a human being, someone who can be forthright one moment and secretive the next, someone who is hopeful one moment and demoralized the next, just like you. Get ready — your species is waiting.

EXERCISES

Easy. Say, "People come with a personality, and that's okay."

Easy. Say, "People come with anxieties and moods, and that's okay."

Medium. Picture yourself arriving to be coached. Who has arrived?

High bar. Picture a hypothetical client scenario where you are working with a self-identified anxious client. How might you work with her? What might you suggest? What do you need to learn for yourself about anxiety management that would help you better support your clients who present with anxiety?

Food for Thought for Informal Coaches

Do you have any particular way of taking into account that the folks you informally coach are coming with a personality, a history, anxieties, and all the rest? How might you better take that into account?

Writing Prompt for Self-Coaches

Write to the prompt "I understand that I bring all of the following to the table..."

62

A Single Session

A single session, whether it's the first session or some subsequent
session, is — or can be — a beautiful thing. If the human brain
is the most complicated bit of matter in the known universe, and if
human beings are the most intricate of known life-forms, then two
brains and two life-forms sitting together working on making life a
little better for one of those life-forms must be one of the universe's
really amazing interactions.

And a session can also be as dull as dishwater. There will be
days when your client doesn't really want to be there. There will
be days when you aren't fully there. Coaching sessions can and will
run the gamut from brilliant to pedestrian. About what isn't this
true? Much of life fits the contours of a normal distribution curve,
with the bulk of whatever is being measured falling in the vast, ordinary middle. This is as true of restaurants, poetry, and dentists as
it is of coaching sessions.

Relax into the belief that there will be many excellent coaching
sessions in your future and that every session, even the dull and
dreary ones, are still serving your clients, just so long as you come
to the session intending to be of help and just so long as you lean
forward and stay engaged. Simply by virtue of leaning forward and
staying engaged, you will provide your client with felt support.
She will feel warmed by the attention you are paying her, by your

concern for her best interests, and by your willingness to be honest, direct, and forthright when some truth telling is required.

Think of yourself as a country doctor who makes house calls. You get to be of some real help, and you also get a glimpse into a person's real life, including the facts that the dishes are piled a bit high in the sink and the chickens are looking awfully scrawny. Like that country doctor of olden times, you are almost part of the family, part friend, part professional, frank and trustworthy, with the know-how to make even a brief visit valuable. On some visits, that country doctor might say nothing more than, "Remember to take your heart medicine." And that reminder will be helpful.

Sometimes you will work with a client for exactly a single session. If you come to that session relaxed, create some quality quiet, ask some quality questions, help your client articulate his goals and name the action steps that serve those goals, cheerlead for hope and possibility, and end the session with a bit of a summary that your client can take with him as marching orders, that will be about as good a half hour, forty-five minutes, or hour as two people can spend together.

In my own practice, I schedule five client sessions a day on client days. These forty-five minute sessions are back-to-back, with fifteen minutes in between them. If these sessions amounted to heavy lifting, five sessions in a row would constitute an exhausting amount of work. But I am merely normally tired at the end of those five sessions, as anyone might be having done some real work, rather than drained or exhausted. I hope that you will have a similar experience. In the beginning, you may not be able to do several sessions back-to-back; but if you can learn to coach easy, that time will come.

EXERCISES

Easy. Say, "A single session can be a beautiful thing."

Easy. Say, "Each session is an event, an experience, and an adventure."

Medium. Sometimes time seems to move slowly, as when you are watching the clock. Sometimes time seems to move quickly, as when you are fully engrossed in something. Picture sessions as engrossing encounters that move along at quite a nice clip. Keep that feeling and that picture in mind when you think about sessions.

High bar. If you aren't currently coaching clients, enlist a volunteer client or two and do some practice but real sessions. The best way to learn what sessions feel like is to have some!

Food for Thought for Informal Coaches

When you informally coach, do you usually know how much time the two of you will have together? If you don't, might it be useful to begin to schedule even informal sessions a little formally, so that you know when a session is due to end and when it's time to summarize a bit?

Writing Prompt for Self-Coaches

Write to the prompt "I think I would like to create self-coaching sessions that…"

63

Working Together

If you imagine that you are doing all the work, as a doctor might as he examines a patient, you may find coaching rather hard. But if you imagine that you and your client are working together, as two soccer players work together, passing the ball back and forth on the way to the goal, you will experience coaching as a much easier thing and even as a beautiful thing.

Those two teammates are actually enjoying themselves. Yes, the championship may depend on how well they play, the stakes may be very high, their reputations may be on the line, and they may be taking the moment very seriously indeed. But they are also deeply enjoying the unspoken communication between them, their sense of shared momentum, their literal forward progress, and their ability to create a beautiful thing between them.

Coaching can be like that. You and your client are working together on both stated goals and unstated goals, just as those two soccer players are. The soccer players' obvious goals are to score and to win. But they are also involved in something that is at the heart of sports — the beautiful passes, the split-second decisions, the way you can kick a ball and thread a needle. All of those are the unspoken bits. Likewise, in coaching, you and your client are working ostensibly on, say, getting her documentary made. But you are also working on the unspoken matters, reminding her of her love of film, helping her better tolerate solitude, and all the rest.

You might work with a given client for a single session, for a number of sessions, or even for years. In my own coaching practice, I tend to work with clients for a year, as my most popular package offers one year of coaching. But I also work with many clients for just a single session, often because that is all that is needed at that moment. In that one session, I may be able to help a client move all the way from confusion to clarity, from ambivalence to resolve, and from despair to a measure of restored hope.

This is possible in one session only because my client was already prepared to go there. I didn't drag him to that better place kicking and screaming, which would have been impossible, anyway. He came to me ready to be helped and ready to be of help. He came to work, to work together with me. Imagine if I were one of those soccer players and I had to drag my teammate onto the field and somehow make him play. That couldn't happen. He'd have to run onto the field of his own accord — exactly as do our clients.

Clients may be nervous, uncertain, skeptical, but they have run onto the field. They have come willing, if not necessarily eager, to work. Will we work together brilliantly? Sometimes. In life, we have our share of effective and ineffective collaborations and better and worse experiences of working with other people. The same is true of coaching. But, on balance, you will have many more positive experiences of working together than duds. You can count on that!

Coaching is relational. There is an objective — your client's stated goal — just as there may be the goal of scoring in soccer or of building a bridge to connect two townships separated by a river. Such objectives are able to be achieved only because people can work together. Imagine if people never could work together — where would we be? Fortunately, we can. Coaching is proof of that. You and your client are a version of a championship team.

Easy. Say, "My clients and I can work together beautifully."

Easy. Say, "Coaching is not about heavy lifting or working alone."

Medium. Picture your client and yourself leaning back and widening the distance between you. Now picture the two of you leaning forward, narrowing the distance between you, and working together. Can you describe the felt difference between the one and the other?

High bar. Imagine a hypothetical client scenario where the two of you are working together beautifully. Picture that experience and enjoy that experience.

Food for Thought for Informal Coaches

When you informally coach, do you have the sense that the two of you are working together? If you don't have that sense, what might be missing from those informal coaching relationships?

Writing Prompt for Self-Coaches

Write to the prompt "Given that I'm self-coaching and not working with someone else, I'm going to translate the idea of working together into the following…"

64

Session Magic

When I first started working with clients thirty-five or so years ago as a family therapist, every session was a bit of an ordeal. Individuals, and sometimes couples and families, brought me their darkest moods and their boiling feuds. I thought I was supposed to fix everything, all in the context of a suspect "diagnose and treat" model. It took only a short time for me to abandon that "mental disorder" model and take off my invisible white coat. But it took a lot of time, meaning years, to find sessions easy; and it took a lot of time, also meaning years, to become human in session.

Making the transition to coaching helped a lot. As a licensed family therapist, I was rather obliged to look for mental disorders and rather obliged to apply the diagnosing and treating language of medicine. In that lane, I was a putative expert. Transitioning to coaching allowed me to come down off that pedestal, smile a bit, and chat with clients as one person to another. Shifting to the much less prestigious but much more appropriate coaching model, where my clients and I could just talk frankly about goals and the efforts required to meet those goals, helped a lot.

And magic happens when two people actually talk. Most conversations are superficial or informational — that's all they need to be. You ask your kids if they want grilled cheese sandwiches or fish sticks for dinner. There's not much more to say. Your husband lets you know when his plane is landing. That's the information you need. Your friend tells you about a restaurant that she enjoyed, rather than burdening you with the details of her rocky marriage. That may be exactly how both of you want that chat to go, as neither of you may be inclined to get into the weeds of real life at that moment.

But if your friend sighs and says, "Do you mind if I tell you what's been going on with Jim?" everything changes. You nod, accepting the demands and responsibilities of friendship and adulthood. You grow very quiet — that quality quiet we've discussed. You prepare yourself to be of help, whether that help is you sympathizing, assisting your friend as she tries to tease apart what's really going on, or problem-solving, as in discussing what she will do if Jim bullies or threatens her again. The second your friend announces that she would like to have a real conversation with you, the atmosphere in the room changes.

This is rather extraordinary, that it is possible for two friends to be talking one minute about that new Thai restaurant that opened down the block and the next minute about domestic violence. We are that sort of species, able to do either, and that the latter is possible, that two people can move from the superficiality and banality of everyday conversation to a serious, life-affecting place in the blink of an eye, is what makes coaching both possible and remarkably valuable.

No preambles are necessary. No sets of instructions are required. All that is needed is the unspoken agreement that real work is about to commence. Just like that, you and your client are *right there*, holding the beating heart of the matter in your four hands. Isn't that quite something?

EXERCISES

Easy. Say, "I can see how sessions are rather magical."

Easy. Say, "Being with another person in serious conversation is one of life's amazing experiences."

Medium. Picture that remarkable thing, two people facing each other, being serious together. Enjoy that image. That is at least as beautiful and magical as a glorious sunset or a shady glen, wouldn't you say?

High bar. Play with the distinction between coaching as work or coaching as a profession and the idea of coaching as human magic. What thoughts and feelings come up for you as you consider the phrase "coaching as human magic"?

Food for Thought for Informal Coaches

Say that you are informally coaching your child about an upcoming performance at school. Can you feel how that chat is both practical and magical? Does the phrase "practical magic" resonate for you?

Writing Prompt for Self-Coaches

Write to the prompt "Coaching myself is different from the other things that I do, like reading a book or chatting with friends. It is special because…"

65

When the Help Has Helped

In working with creative and performing artists for decades, I've come to learn the extent to which they remember the criticisms they've received and forget their successes. If 75 percent of the reviews of their latest concert are positive and 25 percent are negative, they are likely to feel as if their concert has been raked over the coals. Human beings seem to be built this way, to put much more store in the criticism they receive than in the praise.

The same is true for coaches. A coach may have helped four folks on a given day and had a less than stellar session with a fifth person and decided to take that less than stellar session to bed with her. In such ways do we skew our vision of how life is going. It's important that a coach celebrate all those good sessions, because it is no small thing to have actually helped another human being. If you don't stop to notice that your help has helped, you may find yourself judging your coaching negatively and even harshly. Let the good sessions count!

Coaches really can help. A client may come in with multiple high bar goals, from finally beginning his first novel to finding a better day job to improving his relationship with his wife to reducing his compulsive internet surfing to making peace with his elderly authoritarian father. With your help, he may gain some traction on *all* these goals. He may not only begin his novel but finish it; he may discover that the peace to be made with his father is possible only by completely avoiding him; he may begin to make the transition from employee to self-employed entrepreneur. That is a lot!

Each will likely be an imperfect solution: his novel may be finished, but not to his liking; he may harbor some guilt about giving up on his relationship with his father; he may discover just how hard it is to run a one-person business and resign himself to the necessity of a salary. These are the human-sized results that we get when we work with human beings. But it is not nothing that he started and finished his novel. It is not nothing that he found the way to make some peace with his father. It is not nothing that he finally faced the rigors and realities of starting a business. You may not have worked miracles, but you have really helped, and he will genuinely appreciate the effort you made.

And sometimes the help can prove dramatically valuable. I've had clients amaze themselves by reaching their high bar goals, goals that had seemed quite fantastical and completely out of reach. You, too, will have experiences of this sort, if you decide to coach. On a given day, you will be of some help; and occasionally the results will be dramatic. And, yes, there will be days when your client is down, unmotivated, overwhelmed, and feeling pretty hopeless — and even then, you can help, by listening, by offering some kindness and some consolation, and by being human. That, too, is a beautiful session.

EXERCISES

Easy. Say, "I would enjoy coaching."

Easy. Say, "I can learn to coach easily and effortlessly."

Medium. If you are already a coach and if this is the right moment for you to recommit to coaching, create a little ceremony of recommitment. If you aren't already a coach but would like to begin, create a little ceremony of initiation as you open a door, cross a threshold, and take some steps in the direction of beginning.

High bar. If you are currently a coach but haven't yet fully committed to coaching, let this be the moment you commit. Create an action plan for building your coaching business and follow through on that plan. If you aren't a coach yet but would like to begin, take this opportunity to figure out your first steps, which might involve undergoing a training, enrolling in a coaching program, or offering informal coaching in your circle and networks.

Food for Thought for Informal Coaches

What are the main takeaways from this book that you might put to use in the informal coaching work that you do?

Writing Prompt for Self-Coaches

Write to the prompt "I now have a picture of what self-coaching might look like. It might look like..."

About the Author

Eric Maisel, PhD, is the author of more than fifty books in the areas of creativity, the creative life, coaching, life purpose and meaning, writing, and critical psychology and critical psychiatry. His books include *Fearless Creating*, *Coaching the Artist Within*, *The Power of Daily Practice*, *Why Smart People Hurt*, and *Redesign Your Mind*.

Dr. Maisel, widely regarded as America's foremost creativity coach, is a retired psychotherapist, active creativity coach, and critical psychology advocate. He writes the *Rethinking Mental Health* blog for *Psychology Today*, with three-million-plus views; lectures nationally and internationally; and delivers keynotes for organizations like the International Society for Ethical Psychology and Psychiatry and the American Mental Health Counselors Association. He created and is the lead editor for the Ethics International Press Critical Psychology and Critical Psychiatry Series.

Dr. Maisel has facilitated deep writing workshops in locations like Paris, London, New York, Dublin, Prague, and Rome, provided reporters with hundreds of print, radio, and television interviews, and taught tens of thousands of students through his online classes. You can learn more about his workshops, trainings, books, and services at EricMaisel.com and more about Kirism, the contemporary philosophy of life that he has developed, at Kirism.com.

Author's Note

Please feel free to be in touch with me at ericmaisel@hotmail.com or visit me at EricMaisel.com. I offer creativity coaching trainings, mastering the coaching session trainings, individual coaching, and more. Come visit!

For a full description of my fifty-plus books, please visit my website. I look forward to hearing from you and possibly working with you in the future.